# LEADERSHIP EQUANIMITY

The New Super Skill for Leaders

DR. JENNIFER SIGNE CARD

Leadership Equanimity: The New Super Skill for Leaders
Copyright © 2023 by Dr. Jennifer Signe Card

All rights reserved. No part of this publication may be reproduced, distributed, or transmitted in any form or by any means, including photocopying, recording, or other electronic or mechanical methods, without the prior written permission of the author, except in the case of brief quotations embodied in critical reviews and certain other non-commercial uses permitted by copyright law.

tellwell

Tellwell Talent
www.tellwell.ca

ISBN
978-0-2288-8849-9 (Hardcover)
978-0-2288-8062-2 (Paperback)
978-0-2288-8851-2 (eBook)

# TABLE OF CONTENTS

Introduction .................................................. xiii

Chapter 1   **Equanimity** ............................... 1
- What is Equanimity?
- How can it help Leadership?

Chapter 2   **Inner Wisdom** ......................... 9
- Self-Awareness and Leadership

Chapter 3   **De-Stressing** .......................... 14
- How Equanimity Helps to Neutralize Stress
- Psychological Self-Care For Leaders

Chapter 4   **Finding Calm** ........................ 31
- Mindfulness
- Nature As A Psychological Nurturer

Chapter 5   **Perspective** ............................ 41
- Growth Mindset
- SISU

Chapter 6   **Choosing Happiness** ............ 50
- Emotions and Equanimity
- Personal Mantras

Chapter 7   **Mind Agility** ......................... 58
- Biases & Thinking Errors
- Resilience

Chapter 8   **How to Befriend Change** ..... 69
- Tolerance for Ambiguity

Chapter 9    **SPACE4EQ** ............................................ **79**
- Self-Affirmation
- Inner Linguistics

Chapter 10    **Communication and Equanimity** ....... **92**
- Navigating Conflict
- Listening

Chapter 11    **The Equanimous Leader** ................... **101**

About the Author ....................................................... 107
Notes ....................................................................... 109

# TESTIMONIALS

*"In the volatile, uncertain, complex and ambiguous world of work today, equanimity is not only a super-power, but a super-necessity for leaders. Dr. Card brings together a unique blend of principles, examples and how-to reflections, in a quick, easy to read book. I will be giving it to all my clients."*

*Catherine Kemmerling, PsyD, MEd,*
*The Resilience Retreat Center*

*As leader: Are you addicted to a high level of busyness? Do you (subconsciously) believe you need to work hard or hardest to be effective? Or be the expert in everything? Do you have a hard time to give yourself permission to make space to think and feel? Then this book is for you. Jennifer Card makes a meaningful and actionable contribution to the concept of equanimity: the capacity for self-composure, self-awareness, and cognitive calmness in the face of uncertainty. A superpower for any leader in a time of rising uncertainty and ever more complexity.*

*Katharina Schmidt, PsyD, MBA, Executive Coach,*
*Inspiration & Discipline*

"As I read this book, I can positively reframe many of the challenges that are most nagging in my leadership role. The examples help the reader to see that equanimity can be gained through small moments, not grandiose gestures. The exercises and reflections offer insight into ways to live what you learn as you read."

*Suzanne Devlin, PhD, Chair,*
*Organizational and Leadership Psychology Department,*
*William James College*

"We all want to perform at our best. The reality, though, is that we spend much of our time off balance, drained, and operating in survival mode. Dr. Card's book provides an antidote to this common experience. While developing traditional leadership skills is important, Dr. Card guides and equips leaders to cultivate the meta-skill of equanimity, which in turn unleashes one's best self. Today's leaders must adopt a "marathon" mindset and skill set. Leadership Equanimity is the instruction manual that will carry leaders across the finish line with energy to spare."

*Dr. Elias Ursitti,*
*Leadership Psychologist and Executive Coach*

"Leadership Equinimity provides leaders with an easy-to-follow plan for developing a powerful internal framework necessary for navigating the complexities of the changing world and one that can guide them through the difficult decisions and unexpected challenges therein. Drawing on insights from *positive psychology, organizational psychology, neuroscience, and mindfulness training, Dr. Card gives readers a comprehensive understanding of the power and potential of equanimity. Its lessons are invaluable and have helped me become a more reflective, mindful, and compassionate leader while equipping me with vital tools necessary for helping my clients find their own inner harmony."*

Dr. Matthew Dunn,
Organizational Sport Psychologist & Performance Coach,
Performance Rising

"The insights in this book help leaders become the well-being hub of their organizations by first cultivating their power over their own minds. Dr. Card's theory-based and practice-oriented methods are universally applicable to leaders across geographic regions, times, professional fields, seniority levels, and challenges; every leader can find a home in this book."

Ravit Heskiau, PhD, Associate Teaching Professor,
D'Amore-McKim School of Business,
Northeastern University

# DEDICATION

To my husband Duncan, my kiddos Baillie,
J.D. & Beau, my mum and dad Judy & John,
my sister Kim, and rescue dog Chipper.

*Kiitos*

# DISCLAIMER

Please note that I do not make any guarantees about the results of the information, suggestions or guidance I provide in this book. I have shared educational and informational resources that are intended to help you navigate the challenging waters of leadership development. Leadership coaching and related advice can only be provided in the context specific fact situations and each circumstance requires unique and customized approaches to facilitate successful outcomes. The content of this book is general in nature and must not be relied on or used as a substitute for leadership coaching advice that is secured from a qualified, trained and competent advisor. Your ultimate success or failure will be the result of your particular situation and innumerable other circumstances that are beyond my knowledge and control.

Leadership Equanimity: The New Super Skill for Leaders and How to Cultivate It

**Introduction**

*"When the force of circumstance upsets your equanimity, lose no time in recovering your self-control, and do not remain out of tune longer than you can help. Habitual recurrence to the harmony will increase your mastery of it." –Marcus Aurelias, AD*

As I work with leaders across all sectors, I hear the ubiquitous refrain that they wish they had more time to strategize, think, regroup, feel less stressed, and simply catch their breath. Their calendars are saturated, and the information overload can sometimes be unbearable, especially with the continued uncertainty. How can leaders feel less stressed, triage their priorities, find more space in their calendars, and navigate uncertainty with greater ease? I propose that the answer is equanimity.

The term equanimity might have one conjuring an image of a monk meditating, perhaps near a lily pond, or one may think it has something to do with yoga. Traditionally, equanimity is the state of maintaining mental calmness and composure especially during moments of turmoil, stress and disruption. I believe *contemporary* equanimity for leaders and in the workplace doesn't necessarily mean being *Zened* out, but instead, more aligned with what Marcus Aurelias alluded to: being able to recover one's composure even after being "rocked" by external forces and holding this calm-minded perspective in the face of ongoing challenge.

With the super skill of equanimity, a leader could be less stressed by external events, more comfortable with change and challenge, and less distracted by unnecessaries. An equanimous mind is more equipped to depersonalize a situation, reduce personal triggers, and be more mindful of the entirety of each moment, just as it is and for what it is.

Contemporary equanimity is a skill set that requires cultivation and prework. It would be challenging to suddenly be equanimous without first having created the mental space for it to occur. A stressed-out and distracted mind does not have room for calmness and composure. A stressed-out mind is too busy worrying about the future and ruminating about the past to be present. Equanimity starts with practicing good mental hygiene or psychological self-care, similar to physical self-care; both increase the capacity for improved performance.

> ***Equanimity is the balance of co-holding the external and internal views in a separated and supple dance so that you are empowered to selectively apply your full awareness to the moment with acceptance and depersonalization.***

With saturated calendars and information overload, leaders need more *think-time* and reaction-time, which I like to refer to as SPACE4EQ (space for equanimity). SPACE4EQ can help create more mind-room to reflect, make decisions, synthesize and tirage information, think strategically, and psychologically self-care. SPACE4EQ is akin to gaining more mental real estate between a triggering event (demands) and one's chosen reactions (resources). Synthesizing complex situations requires rapid processing time, quick mental downloads of data, and a sense of detachment from the moment, all while being present in the moment for perspective—this is equanimity.

Contemporary equanimity for leaders also aligns with the perspective-enhancing concept of being able to *co-hold* the tension of both the external world and its demands with the internal world of self-awareness of thoughts and feelings. Leader equanimity could be akin to mindfulness in action because it enables leaders to untether from external stressors, focus attention on the present moment, be less distracted by unnecessary mind-clutter, find a greater amount of reaction time between oneself and the moment, have more clarity to triage information effectively and make decisions with a calmer-head.

Leader equanimity is about being the captain of one's sailboat; the sailboat may not be void of external pressures, tension, challenge, or complexity (aka Mother Nature), but it can maintain its balance. In fact, it captures the external tensions or wind force and channels it for increased power; the co-holding of the tension of the external and internal might even fuel the sailboat's speed on its course with focused, not wasted, energy.

As an organizational and leadership psychologist, I am fascinated by the human experience, particularly the human experience while at work. Our brains are powerful and shape so much of our reality; once a leader can become aware of how they are thinking, feeling, and reacting, especially in the moment, they will become better equipped to center themselves and their teams.

For several years, I have been researching the psychology of leadership, with a focus on leader well-being. While there is abundant research and literature on how to increase a leader's physical well-being through sustained practices such as nutrition and exercise, much less research has been undertaken to identify the ways to improve the *psychological* well-being of leaders. In a sense, that may surprise some because we all know that one of the greatest threats to a leader's overall well-being is stress, which is so often contagious within an organization. So, it is a simple rational truth that if we confront and deal with how a leader reacts to stressful situations, we can improve their psychological well-being and performance.

As mentioned previously, stress occurs when our demands exceed available resources. This can happen at the physical level, for example, during weightlifting, when the demand of the bench press might become too great for the available power of the muscle. This can happen at the psychological level when cognitive and attention demands start to burden and surpass available resources (such as *time to think*). The argument in this equation would be to simply lessen demands and increase resources, to which I agree, but the reality is that this is not always possible, but there is hope. I think that the perception of demands might shift the equation, and so too could the development of equanimity and psychological self-care to increase available cognitive resources.

Increasing psychological well-being is the first and critical step to expanding psychological reserves, similar to that of our physical bodies. A fit body has much more energy and flexibility to perform, and a fit mind could do the same. Now, here is the double positive: as we practice good mental hygiene and psychological self-care, it could result in greater SPACE4EQ, or in otherwords, space for equanimity, which would feed back into a positive loop.

With continued competing demands and complexities, one of the important things to embrace in this new non-normal is perspective, focus, and awareness, which speaks to equanimity. Equanimity, in my opinion, is going to continue to grow as a super skill for the future. Equanimity allows you to mindfully focus on the present NOW, not ruminate on the past or worry about the future, while simultaneously enabling you to tune in to the moment and how you and others are feeling.

The balancing aspect of leader equanimity provides a space for tolerance because it helps one to co-hold the tension of the environment with the tension of one's mind. When there is room or capacity in one's mind to co-hold competing tensions, there is room for more tolerance of the other and the environment, increased personal awareness, ownership, and acceptance—and a broader grasp of grace and ease. Equanimity is the ability to co-hold the view of both the forest and the trees in an engaged yet untangled way.

I remember once asking the chairman of a massive multinational how they handled the responsibility, and their response was, "I don't worry, but I remain concerned." This comment always stuck with me in its differentiation and depersonalization, yet its balanced way of engagement: respect for the self and the environment. Concern is different from worry. I would bet that concern does not get internalized in the same volume nor inflict the same level of stress.

Contemporary leadership equanimity involves the psychological capacity to be self-aware and mentally anchored from within. Alternatively, when a leader is anchored to external forces, especially in today's world of volatility and uncertainty, they are less likely to have the inner control required to recover. However, being an equanimous leader requires proactive work to be prepared and ready for challenges and uncertainty. It's *not* about being an expert of the knowable; it's about being an expert of your inner ability to find your composure, be open to learning, and be mentally supple to expand your perspective. One of the measurables of being physically fit is the ability of a quick recovery. So too is that of psychological fitness and equanimity.

Our physical bodies love to be fit; it feels good to have the reserves and the flexibility, and the same goes for our mental fitness. It feels good to have inner mind harmony, not get thrown off by external triggers, and recover quickly.

Leader equanimity is not only an important outcome of increased psychological self-care, but it is also a contemporary *way of being* in response to changing external environments. The very definition of leadership is changing, as are the requirements. Being a leader, any kind of leader, including being a parent, head of a multinational, or leading yourself, is becoming more complex as our universe continues to sway in new ways.

No longer is a leader defined by being the expert or having the most seniority, highest authority, or even all of the answers. As our experiences exponentially morph into unforeseen patterns of reality, the top-down leadership equation no longer makes sense. In fact, it might even topple with the ongoing sways of our present day.

Leadership today requires an open door, inclusivity, meaningful conversations, and dynamic approaches. Leadership has become more of a learn-as-you-go. There is too much complexity and change for leaders to be static or experts. In fact, it's a waste of time. It is similar to how education is evolving; memorizing information has become irrelevant with the computer age and, almost, unlimited access to information. Instead, it's more about the ability to process, discern, research, and digest information.

To some extent, leadership used to be about offering a sense of control, stability, and regularity to the environment, but with the new universe of constant pivoting and adapting, this is no longer possible. Now, the focus is shifting internally into the minds, behaviours, and adaptability of leaders. While a leader may no longer be able to control the environment, they can empower themselves with self-knowledge, psychological resources, and the ability to anchor themselves from within. This empowerment, I equate to equanimity.

> ***When a leader can find their inner balance, they will be better prepared to navigate the uncharted and choppy waters.***

Equanimity is an ancient concept, but its tenets hold true for the modern era. Also important to note is that equanimity does not necessarily involve resolving or dissolving opposing tensions but holding their balance. This is an important distinction when dealing with complexity.

Cultivating the super skill of equanimity requires reserves, especially psychological reserves, and mental suppleness. Just like a marathoner needs physical reserves, leaders need psychological reserves gained from more than just a day at the spa. Reserves take nourishment, like a garden needs to be cultivated. The freedom to use such reserves at will is only available to those who have more than just a last drop in the bucket, otherwise grit and fortitude would have to kick in to deplete its contents. When we have plenty of reserves in our metaphorical bucket we can dip in as we need to without feeling the impact. Conscious wellbeing and self-care can help to sustain and refill these buckets or reserves.

Leader equanimity requires the positive antecedent of psychological well-being and know-how. This book is about cultivating equanimity through mental well-being as a first response. When a leader develops a daily regime of healthy micro mind habits and SPACE4EQ, and is armed with a set of navigational tools, they will be better equipped to steer the ship through uncharted waters while not burning themselves out. Burnout does not happen overnight, nor does psychological self-care as a counter.

As a matter of leadership culture in our society, leaders too often hit the "stress reaction" button internally when maybe they don't have to. But, like leaders, we should all save this *stress reaction energy* for when it matters. So, how can we best understand when triaging stress triggers matter?

Answer: equanimity. Equanimity is a superpower that can stretch a stressful event's processing time; help us not be unnecessarily reactive; and increase the capacity to process stressful situations in a greater untethered way. Equanimity for leaders (in the workplace) is about arriving at the "office" armed with the capacity and the psychological reserves to remain untriggered and with a view of the bigger picture that allows a leader to be more "in the moment." The more in the moment you can be, the less worry you will have about the future, and the less you will ruminate about the past, thus freeing up valuable real estate in your mind to do much more valuable things. Increased SPACE4EQ allows for the practice of: being more focused *on* the moment, being more self-aware *in* the moment, and being more conscious *of* the moment.

> ***Equanimity is elevated mindfulness in action. It is the catalyst for freedom of thought and perspective.***

My intention:

We live in a stress-fulfilling society. The proof is evident by simply turning on the evening news to observe the polarization, divisiveness, and heightened world. My hope is to help leaders (humans!) fill their psychological reserve buckets so they can expand their resources and then outsmart demands. Hence, the changed psychological stress equation equalling more psychological well-being. This increase in psychological well-being could improve the chances of practicing more equanimity.

In addition, the conversation around stress as a *badge of honor* for leaders needs to change. While bits of stress aren't necessarily harmful, even motivating at times (I personally love a good deadline and a little pressure!), prolonged and chronic psychological stress is. Chronic stress is harmful to a leader's well-being, performance, and happiness. I wonder if, as a society, we have forgotten how to *not* be stressed and could all use a little more inner harmony. Inner harmony, composure, tolerance, empathy, adaption, and clarity are just a few of the bi-products of equanimity.

Take a second to envision a leader from your past that inspired you. I'll bet that they were equanimous. They had a palpable composure, and their grounding energy was like gravity to the organization. Throughout history, the real positive change agents (leaders!) have embodied elements of equanimity. A hurricane could be around them, but you knew they were *still* inside. Once leaders can stand still and anchor in their inner knowing, they become empowered.

It is my wish that you find this book useful and use it as a path to finding more *SPACE4EQ* to develop more equanimity for yourself and your organization.

> ***Being able to find your inner harmony in the heart of a storm or find** equanimity *is a superpower in today's ever-changing world.***

# CHAPTER 1

# Equanimity

- What is Equanimity?
- How can it help Leadership?

*"We are drowning in information while starving for wisdom. The world henceforth will be run by synthesizers, people able to put together the right information at the right time, think critically about it, and make important choices wisely." –E.O. Wilson*

We live in a stress-fulfilling society in which stress has become normalized, and a sense of peace is a luxury. When was the last time you felt you could pause to catch your breath and quiet your mind as a leader?

Leaders today are required to think critically and synthesize information rapidly while continually using sound judgement; this all requires the *superpower and mind skill* of equanimity. By definition, equanimity is the capacity for self-composure, self-awareness, and cognitive (mind) calmness, especially while under pressure. In practice, equanimity is the ability to pause, self-reflect on the fly, regroup, and be clear in the heart of the storm.

Equanimity also stretches the space before your reaction time by offering you a *gap* to check in with yourself, your reactions, your observations, and your decisions. The space of equanimity allows you to be more intentional and less reactional, a super skill needed by leaders today.

> ***Equanimity is about holding the entire picture in view, even in the face of crisis.***

Equanimity is not about being devoid of any emotions; instead, it is more aligned with the ability to be completely aware of and in balance with your emotions and thoughts.

Equanimity provides the empowerment to synthesize what's going on around you, with the internal *space* to respond intentionally rather than react. With the constant bombardment of uncertainty and challenge as a leader, equanimity could offer an inner harmony to be *less rocked* by circumstance.

> ***There is freedom in the control of consciously choosing how you react both internally and externally. Otherwise, you are your reaction's prisoner.***

Arguably, some people, whether culturally engrained or just genetically gifted, find equanimity easier; however, it is important to note that it can be cultivated—that is what this book is about. I've gathered research from positive psychology, organizational psychology, neuroscience, and mindfulness training to provide a *how-to* for cultivating more equanimity.

Equanimity is a continuum for most unless you are a monk or a saint! Some days or in some contexts, you will likely feel more at peace with yourself and your world, while other days can feel like more of a struggle. Hopefully, this book will help you to identify the accelerators and resistors to your inner calm. Research helps point the way, too. For example, extensive research indicates that nature is a mind nurturer, and meditation increases awareness and the ability to be present. When you are truly present, you are not ruminating about the past or worrying about the future, which impacts your reaction levels in the moment.

I like to equate equanimity to the eye of a hurricane. After years of living in Bermuda, I experienced some very powerful hurricanes, one, in particular, was a category four hurricane that lasted over eight hours, and the eye travelled precisely over the island. The power of the wind felt like a high-speed train hammering through our house, full noise and vibration. The scariest thing about a hurricane is the level of uncertainty: will the tide get so high that it will rush into my home? Will my windows implode? Will a tornado plow through my house? I had all these thoughts while various things were bombing our roof (including our fence posts).

In the middle of the hurricane, it was amazing to experience being in the eye of it. After four hours of a full-speed train, there was a sudden absolute dead calm and pitch quiet. We quickly went outside to see a clear sky full of stars. Even the tree frogs started to chirp. The eye was like an oasis in the desert. It's hard to imagine that it exists. The peace and quiet after the train ride allowed us to catch our breath to prepare for the back side of the hurricane, which would be another four hours. As storms will persist in life, especially in leadership, pulling yourself into the calm of the eye is a super skill for survival and success.

Being equanimous as a leader allows you to *choose* your response while under stress so as not to get overwhelmed by it. The Dalai Lama asserts that equanimity allows a person to not "fall into extreme states of the mind… allowing you to be free from being caught up in the play of emotions."[1] Having the mind power of equanimity does not mean that a leader always has to deploy it or that highly emotional reactions are not permitted or are inappropriate, but it does mean that a leader has the psychological power of choice in their reaction and the ability to use equanimity to rebalance.

**Equanimity in Action**

As an example, let's compare EQ Elliott with Reactive Rob. Both are leaders at a technology company, and both have just discovered that the software their team has been developing (all year) has a glitch, so it can't launch on schedule. We all know how Reactive Rob is going to respond to the news. There will be blame, there will be possible yelling, there will be potential firing, and there will be more pressure put on an already stressed-out team.

On the contrary, let's look at EQ Elliott. The minute he hears the news, Elliott takes a moment of quiet, goes out for a quick walk to get some fresh air, steadies his mind, and takes a few good deep breaths. EQ Elliott pulls the team into a meeting, congratulates them on their hard work, and reminds them that technology isn't created overnight and that errors can point to opportunities. EQ Elliott then allows the team to express their shared frustrations and disappointments and then asks the team, "What do you think we should do now?" EQ Elliott expresses relief that the software was not yet deployed. The team immediately starts brainstorming to identify the glitch, and inevitably, they end up with a superior software.

EQ Elliott has expressed the super skill and inner harmony of equanimity as a leader and turned a mistake into a chance to grow while bringing the team closer and increasing the level of *psychological safety*.[2] Without a doubt, Reactive Rob's team members would have been reluctant to speak up and instead likely to become shut down.

Equanimity, or the ability to keep calm and maintain *untriggered* in the face of adversity, begins with the *prework* outlined in this book. A leader needs to have the psychological fortitude, awareness, and reserves to untether themselves from the grip of stress while maintaining perspective. While the source of the stress may *not* be within your control, your ability to depersonalize a stressor *is*.

The ability to be equanimous includes centering yourself, depersonalizing the situation, and being self-aware of any internal emotional reactions, all while calming them and essentially untangling yourself from the moment. Equanimity provides the space-in-between to pause, reflect, and intentionally choose your reaction.

Equanimity allows you to dig inward and be reflective in action rather than constantly being distracted by external validation of your thoughts.

When you are looking for things external to yourself to appease you, please you, and relieve you, then you are at the mercy of something outside of your control. This is destabilizing and somewhat dangerous. But, when you have the power to find the center within yourself, you are in control of what you can control, which are your reactions, your attitude, and your behaviours.

***Equanimity is about anchoring yourself from within.***

Personally, I used to witness equanimity in my grandmother. She had a small lakeside cottage. Growing up, I would spend a good portion of my summers there, along with a zillion of my other cousins. Her tiny kitchen was always bubbling over with meal preparation and dishwashing. Cats, dogs, and kids ran feral, slamming the sliding door to race to the lake. Looking back, I remember that every day at precisely 11:00 a.m., my grandmother would take a moment to sit quietly at the dining table in the middle of it all with her tea and toast with honey. She engulfed herself with an impenetrable aura, and we knew not to disturb her. I could tell that she could hear us, yet she was taking quiet time. Kids would be running by, screaming fun, and she would slowly butter her toast and enjoy her morning ritual of self-care.

Equanimity isn't about zoning out. It is about zoning in, so much so that you are able to balance your own awareness with your environment in a separated dance. I am quite sure that you have heard the expression "Keep calm and carry on," which is a great idea, yet I am always left wondering, "<u>How</u> do you keep calm?". What has to happen before this decision and behavioural choice? That's what this book is all about. It's the how-to on finding more equanimity in your life and enhancing your role as a leader. We live in a stress-fulfilling society and, in general, have forgotten how not to be stressed and feel at peace in one's own mind.

In addition, leaders need to be mentally strong because there is little tolerance for an uncentered spirit during a crisis. A leader's greatest strength, especially during times of stress, is their mind. This book is structured so that in each chapter, I will discuss how to develop more equanimity and prompt you with a related reflection. Reflection is a chance for you to check in with yourself, reconnect with your purpose and interests, process what is happening in your life, and become more intentional in your modus operandi.

By the end of this book, I hope you will have increased your knowledge of equanimity and the daily practice of being able to reset in the moment and find a sense of inner calm or *wisdom from within* whenever you need it.

Now let's get started.

## **Reflection:**

- Take a moment to think of someone in your world that expresses the superpower of equanimity. How does their equanimity show up? How does their presence make *you* feel?

- Take a moment to think about a time when you were able to harness equanimity. What were the circumstances, and why that moment? How did you feel? How did it change your experience with the challenge?

# CHAPTER 2

# Inner Wisdom

- Self-Awareness and Leadership

*"There is nothing either good or bad, but thinking makes it so." Hamlet,* **William Shakespeare**

Our minds are powerful, yet we spend little time tending to them. Our cognition, or how we think, remember, make decisions, and shape our perspectives directly impacts our reality through our actions and responses. Similar to getting our cars tuned up, we also need to take time to *check in* with ourselves, our thoughts, and our thinking habits. Sometimes our thinking habits need a tune-up too. Like any habit, it can be helpful or counterproductive. Part of this check-in involves exploring things like how and in what way we are using our thinking (our minds) to create our optimal reality. Ultimately, it's about making space for your personal reflection and really getting to know how your mind operates optimally.

Becoming more consciously self-aware of our thinking and reactions is part of mindfulness. True empowerment isn't about control; instead, it is about grounding yourself from within and living from a place of mindful intention.

The self-awareness of mindfulness and is the crux of equanimity, compassion, and empathy (more on this later). Mindfulness is the ability to be completely present and self-aware *of the moment*, and equanimity is the ability to uncouple *from the moment*.

> ***Mindfulness is being-awareness and equanimity is doing-awarenes.***

To see yourself, be yourself, feel yourself, and think for yourself in a sea of slurpy uncertainty is about rising above the moment to truly be free with yourself, your mind, and your reaction from the distraction of reaction.

It is easy and distracting to get swept up in the tides of uncertainty and to automatically jump into problem-solving mode when challenges appear rather than taking a moment to check in and pause to get a better view of the situation. It takes practice to rise above it as an Equanimous Leader for ultimate perspective and stress resiliency.

Uncertainty, and change, even positive change, can spark feelings of unease. The first step to understanding this connection between unease and change is being aware that it can happen as an automatic response. Using mindful and equanimous awareness to reappraise the change may help make the change less uncomfortable which can then help to calm the stress circuitry.

As a leader, being self-aware, mindful, and reflective in the moment can help you to reappraise a situation quickly. Essentially, you enable yourself to **withdraw your reactivity and replace it with intentionality**. The next time you are faced with a challenging situation, take a moment to think about how you are thinking. Your thoughts influence your reality, even when it comes to stress. Essentially, stress does not exist unless you perceive and process it to exist. This is not to suggest that stressful things don't happen, but it does suggest that our reactions are triggered by how we think about things.

With the multitude of chronic distractions, little time is spent thinking about one's thoughts. Getting behind our thinking, in other words, becoming self-aware of our *thinking mind* is part of the equanimous process and tapping into your metacognitive ability. Metacognition is being able to ask yourself in the moment:

- Why am I thinking what I am thinking?
- What is behind my thinking here?
- What is my intention?
- What fears are driving this thinking?
- What biases are at play in how I am thinking?
- What do I truly want in the moment—what's my end game?

Thinking about your thoughts also requires some reflection on your past and culture. How were you raised to think, and in what way? Does your upbringing impact how you think now? How does your thinking align with your values currently? A lack of clarity in your thinking *ways* can sometimes result from a disconnect or incongruence with your values and mission.

For example, let's take a look at fictious Vigilant Veronica. Veronica was raised in a household full of cautious parents who were hypervigilant, which was born out of their need to survive economically. While Veronica never went without food on the table and had the resources to be educated, she was raised to worry about not having, or being, enough—a bit of a scarcity mindset. Veronica's brain is in an almost constant vigilant state.

At work, Veronica is seen as compassionate, fair, and kind as a leader, yet internally, Veronica is constantly worried. Veronica wishes to be free to relax, pursue, and even take risks, but her thoughts criticize and unnecessarily worry about her decisions; the result is that her mind is caught in a struggle.

The more Veronica can become **aware** of her habit of vigilance and its impact on her thinking, the more equipped she becomes to rationalize it before it turns into worry. Sometimes simply knowing and then understanding why we do something helps to lessen the behaviour. Changing a negative habit starts with the mental awareness of the habit.

Perhaps Veronica could reframe her thinking tendency of vigilance and worry as simply concern. Concern, while motivating to action and empathy, is less personalized than worry and helps shift the focus of the internal disruption to then focus the energy toward the external situation.

Being aware of a negative thinking habit, or a tendency to turn concern into worry, is the first step, and then understanding why you default to this tendency is the next step to realizing its potential limitations. Once you become more aware of a negative thinking habit and attune to its limiting impact, you will have a better chance of being motivated to change it.

In the case of Veronica, reflecting on her past is not to be critical of his circumstances but to appreciate and empathize with why it has been influencing how she thinks. This awareness could help her to navigate our thinking tendencies.

***Awareness, Acceptance, Action.***

## **Reflection:**

- Take a moment to reflect on some of your thinking tendencies:
- Under stress, are you an optimist or a worrier? What made you so?
- What situations help you to think at your best? Time of day? Location? Alone? With others?
- Whose thinking abilities do you admire and why?
- What is one thinking habit that you would like to STOP?
- What is one thinking habit that you would like to START?

# CHAPTER 3

# De-Stressing

- How Equanimity Helps to Neutralize Stress
- Psychological Self-Care For Leaders

*"Emancipate yourself from mental slavery, none but ourselves can free our minds!" –Redemption Song by Bob Marley, based on the quote by Marcus Garvey*

I have always appreciated these words because they reflect the fact that so much of our reality is shaped by our minds, and it acknowledges the freedom (and empowerment) to be gained when we can engage in full awareness. Stressful situations are all around us and will likely continue to be, so deciphering which situations are truly threatening and which are not helps create more resiliency to stress. Our brains are wired for protection and vigilance, which is part of our survival, but too often, we react with a greater stress reaction than is required of the situation.

## What is Stress?

As mentioned before, stress occurs when the demand surpasses the available resources to cope. So, technically, in response, there are two ways to deal with stress: either decrease the demand or increase the resources to cope. However, I would add that there is a third way to deal with stress: change the perspective on both the demand and available resources. This is where equanimity comes into play.

I first became interested in the topic of equanimity as a super skill when I began to research psychological self-care and stress resiliency for my doctoral project in graduate school. I would continually read about stress management and relaxation techniques, but I was left thinking that the stress damage and impact had already occurred, hence the word *management*. I then wondered, what if we could change how we perceive something as stressful in the first place? Then there might not be anything to manage or recover from. How could I help leaders (people) initially get in front of certain stress, and what would it take? And what might help someone to reset in the moment or recover faster from a stressful event?

Too often, the stress response resources are deployed when perhaps simply reframing the situation could be enough to change the dynamics. I'm not suggesting that this is the case for every situation or that stress does not exist, but I am suggesting saving your stress-fighting resources for when they are needed, and in the interim, don't let "small" stuff throw you off.

***Become fully aware when you are "under" stress so that you can get "over" it.***

Again, when I say *stress*, I am referring to the chronic and sustained stress, not the momentary stress that blips into your day. Blips of stress pop into your day, and you deal with them and recover. The quieter, chronic and sustained stress that can lead to burnout needs to be addressed. It is important to note that burnout doesn't happen overnight. Instead, cumulative stress piles up inside you until you feel depleted, possibly angry, exhausted, and short-tempered. Burnout is when stress is ahead of you, and your reservers and energy bucket is empty.

Just as burnout doesn't happen overnight, neither does self-care. A quick trip for a massage is great, but it won't erase six months of sustained stress. In addition, while sometimes we need to recover from stress with renewal activities, it is important to try to interrupt the stress before it even takes a toll. Preparing yourself and your reserves to keep stress at arm's length is even better than interrupting the stress.

Equanimity helps to create a pause in between the stimulus and response so that the action or responses chosen are more aligned. Stressful situations will continue to arise, so your psychological capacity to separate yourself from it and to remain within your superpower of equanimity is important; in other words, keeping calm during the storm *if you choose* to. I am not saying that being calm is always the appropriate reaction, nor am I saying that high emotions are not welcome, but I am suggesting that your reactions should be your choice. It doesn't feel good, nor is it helpful, to walk away from a highly emotional reaction sorry about the way in which you engage in it. Your emotions are just that, yours; own them, take charge of them, and get in front of them instead of being at their mercy. Feeling triggered by someone is giving them your power. The same goes for stress. Stress happens, but how you react to it is yours to own.

> ***Burnout does not happen overnight, nor does self-care.***
>
> ***Self-care routines require sustained and intentional actions, similar to a physical fitness routine.***

## Psychological Self-Care and Resiliency

How you (a leader!) process a situation, make decisions, innovate, solve problems, navigate conflict, act on opportunities, assess risk, etc., starts in your mind. The necessary capability for your mind to operate at its full capacity while being able to renew after a stressful event is what I refer to as *psychological self-care*. Psychological self-care is a daily practice of proactively readying the mind for future challenges and knowing how to reset the mind in the moment. Taking care of your greatest asset is similar to taking care of your physical health. It requires attention, know-how, a program, and consistency.

The fact is, your mind does not want to be restricted by the confines of stress; it wants to be free to thrive untethered by triggers, mental distractions, and exhaustion. Psychological self-care gives you the skills to *think* your way out of getting sucked into the vortex of stress. Similar to physical fitness, you cannot just sign up for a marathon and run it successfully. It takes training, sustained attention, rest, recovery, etc. So, too does the well-being of your mind. When your mind is fit and ready, your actions will follow suit.

> ***What you think and how you think will directly impact what you do and how you do it.***

During times of *chronic* stress (not microbursts of stress), a leader's ability to find their centre in the heart of the storm is critical to success. The chances of finding calm in a storm increase when a leader is mentally and physically prepared (or primed) to be ready for action. While available know-how is abundant on physical fitness and body well-being, there is less information on how to train yourself mentally. Mind well-being can be cultivated just like physical fitness, requiring a sustained routine in the same way.

Not only are leaders today finding less time to renew, but they are leaving less time to psychologically self-care as part of that renewal process. In addition, more and more strain is being put on a leader's mind as they face increasing complexity and uncertainty. Similar to physical exhaustion, mental exhaustion can lead to burnout.

Not only can a simple psychological self-care routine be good for you and your performance, but it also impacts your organization because stress and moods are contagious.[1] Knowing that leader stress is contagious to the organization is important, but even more important is how to help leaders prepare for and be resilient to stress before it even happens in the first place; this is called *priming* or preparing oneself for future events. Although being able to recover from stress is important, it is even more important to interrupt the stress response before any damage is done. Increasing your self-awareness to be internally notified when stress is mounting and then knowing what to do to interrupt it will assist with navigating the stressful situation.

**Mind and Body**

While I am a massive proponent of the importance of taking care of the body and understand its interdependent impact on the mind, this relationship is co-dependent. Our well-being is a dance between the psyche (mind) and soma (body). I'll give you a few examples: think of the last time you were exhausted from being in negotiations or dealing with an upset employee. Did you have a headache, or was your body extra fatigued? Could you feel the grip of stress in your body? Or, on a positive note, think of a time when you were engaged in something that you enjoyed, like music or time with friends. Did you feel physically energized as well? It is important to notice when you feel energized, what is about the environment or activity that is contributing to this?

Chronic stress impacts leaders both physically and mentally, but too often, we only care for our bodies. Focusing on psychological self-care is not just about recovery; it is also about the antecedent activities. While not all stress is bad and can even be motivating, sustained stress is harmful to your body, performance, and long-term happiness. Stress can cause a cascade of events in our bodies, including inflammation, sleep disturbances, mental fatigue, hypertension, cardiovascular disease, skin disorders, outbursts, and the list goes on!

> *While stressful events will continue, the impact of stress on a leader can change when your relationship with stress changes.*

After all, stress is a perception, and while there are legitimate stressors, how you process and mentally navigate the stress impacts your reaction and ability to perform. Not always, but sometimes, the stress response can be interrupted with quick and easy interventions (I have included several in this book). In addition to stress interrupters, a leader's mind needs attention, time to renew, and quiet reflection to perform at its best.

Learning how to *untangle* from external stressors, being able to reflect in the moment, becoming aware of personal triggers, and having tools on hand to interrupt the stress response is part of psychological self-care.

Before you get started, I urge you to pull out an *old-school* notebook and pen as your personal reflection journal. Research suggests that writing down your thoughts can reduce your stress level because it helps you surface your thoughts in a reflective manner to process them, depersonalize them, and understand them better.

**The Stress Response**

To understand how to navigate stress, or stress resiliency, let's first review what happens in the body when you perceive something as stressful or a threat. When I mention stress in this book, I will just be referencing psychological stress for leaders at work, not physical stress. Psychological stress for leaders can present in many forms. It can include such things as complexity, adversity, conflict, challenge, change, new experiences, huge learning curves, difficult decisions, tricky negotiations, impactful decisions, buyouts, market slow-downs, new competitors, difficult employees, and the list can go on!

When you perceive something as truly stressful or threatening, your body responds by firing up an area of your brain called the amygdala. With the amygdala fired up, you can then enter into what is commonly known as fight, flight, or freeze mode. Fight, flight, or freeze mode involves changes in your body, such as increased heart rates, blood pressure, breathing rates, etc. Essentially, your body is gearing itself up to flee or fight. While this stress response is a critical survival mechanism to conquer or remove oneself from the threat, what is happening far too often is that one can enter this state unnecessarily when something isn't truly threatening. Think of the unnecessary tole on your body!

When you become chronically stressed, your internal reserves get depleted, so being cognizant of and taking action to calm this stress reaction becomes even harder to do. It becomes a vicious cycle, leading to exhaustion and burnout. This is exactly why priming the Self or filling your personal psychological reserves is important to getting ahead of stress and recovering quickly from it.

Okay, back to psychological reserves and self-care. As a leader, your ability to be primed, ready, and equanimous in the face of adversity can become your superpower. Equanimity is the mental balance and empowerment not to get tangled up with a stressor and to remain removed with a heightened awareness of the Self in the moment. When a stimulus occurs, if you have equanimity, you have the capacity to pause for a moment before you respond, to not only be more intentional about your response behaviour but also buffer yourself from being too tangled up in the perceived stressor or threat. The more you can expand this space and practice, the more it creates a *virtuous*, not vicious, cycle for your well-being and leadership development.

> ***It is a bit of an oxymoron, but there is a freedom in the control of consciously choosing how you respond both internally and externally. Otherwise, you are your reaction's prisoner.***

When you get caught up and constantly triggered by stressful events, you are your reaction's prisoner. Developing the power of equanimity provides you the space to free yourself from triggers and unnecessary reactions.

Let's look at fictious Stressed-out Sam. Sam has always believed that stress makes a person work harder and smarter. Sam believes that being constantly busy is the key to success and that "You can sleep when you retire." Sam loves to be first in the office in the morning, last to go home, and is always training for the next big physical event, such as an ultramarathon. Sure, Sam performs, but the one thing others notice is that Sam never smiles, and any conversation with Sam feels like it has to have a purpose or else you are wasting her time. Sam takes the family on wildly fabulous vacations but spends a good portion of the time on her smartphones, believing that the office "just can't exist without her," when in reality, it's Sam who feels that she can't exist without the office. Sure, Sam will continue to climb in her career, but will she be happy? Will she burn out?

We all know a Stressed-out Sam, and we likely have a bit of Sam in all of us. It is a myth that "Stress gets me charged up." Sure, again, in small doses, but long-term and chronic stress is cognitively distracting and emotionally exhausting, negatively impacting your performance.

One positive side to stress is that it usually exposes a pain point in need of healing, so it could potentially target an opportunity for change and growth. The Chinese symbol for crisis is the balance of danger and opportunity; crisis, stress, and uncertainty can be a starting point for necessary change because it expresses that need. While external crisis and stress are inevitable, your ability to remain calm, mindful, and optimistically engage in these challenges is critical to your mind well-being.

> ***A proactive dance with stress can mitigate its harmful effects.***

Resetting *the way* in which you *see* stressful events while providing psychological self-care interventions on how to prepare for it could be helpful in protecting your well-being. Although life is full of curve balls (and some are doozies!), it's important to remember that stress isn't a beast that lives within you or near you. Instead, stress only exists in your response. Save your energy for when and where it's needed. This is where perspective and resiliency are key.

***If you don't perceive a situation as stressful, then stress doesn't exist.***

Becoming aware of your thoughts and thinking patterns and understanding your biases and triggers helps you to navigate your thoughts and reactions more intentionally. With this *on-demand* self-awareness ability, you can potentially change the way you are thinking, if you need to.

**Are you a Stress-Buncher?**

It is also important to identify unnecessary stress triggers (and we all have them) and avoid what I call *stress-bunching*. Stress triggers may be something unique to you in which you perceive a certain pattern or situation as more threatening than it actually is. World renowned psychiatrist and founding father of cognitive behaviour therapy, Dr. Aaron Beck refers to these as thinking errors, automatic thougths and cognitive distortions.[2] For example, in one area of your life, you might tend to make a mountain out of a molehill, or perhaps you feel like an imposter sometimes. These triggers or thinking errors are cognitive biases that distort the reality of the situation to some degree. Alternatively, it is important to give each moment a chance to be just what it is and no more, in the here and now. Mindfulness is a great way to pull yourself to *this* moment and be fully present by not living in rumination over the past, worrying about the future, or being distorted by biases.

> ***Worry is stressing about something that has never happened. Why bother?***
>
> ***Be vigilant, but don't overindulge to become an unnecessary worry.***

Stress-bunching is when you combine all of your worries and fears into one giant ball and then are left feeling like stress is impacting your entire life. For example, when a client says to me, "My life is too stressful!" I might respond, "Your life, as in your whole life?" To which they usually answer, "Well, no, just this project or person at work." I then ask them, "What is not stressful in your life?"

One area of stress in your life should not permeate the non-stressed areas. I know, easier said than done! But taking a moment to un-bunch the stressor from everything else can help to reduce its resonance. A simple exercise is to draw a giant pie chart and then divide each of the pie pieces into areas of your life such as, friendships, family, hobbies, work, health, finances etc, whatever competing priorities you like, then rate each on a scale of one to ten, with ten being highly stress-causing. Most likely, what you will see is that not all areas of your life are super stressed. (Note, if you rate highly stressed for all or most areas of your life, consider seeking a professional to help or talk to your family doctor because there is great support available.)

When stressed, it is important to identify the root cause and not let it permeate other areas of your life that don't have to be impacted. Stress-bunching lessens your ability to respond appropriately to the issue or threat because it stops you from identifying what actually needs your attention. At the end of your day, your cortisol levels and your mind should be winding down to enter into a restful sleep of renewal. If you are chronically ruminating on something in your mind, even if you are not at work, you will negatively impact this renewal cycle.

Therefore, it is also important to have a wind-down evening routine in place, where you set a boundary between work and home life. It could be something as simple as changing out of your work clothes (or metaphorical or legit uniform!) or taking the dog for a walk as a signal to your body that you are away from work now. As I write this, we are exiting from a global pandemic, and this "away" from work has become even more difficult with home offices. I urge you to also set electronic boundaries with your smartphone and laptop. Unless there is a highly unusual situation, nothing will properly get solved via email at ten minutes to midnight, and it will likely hurt your sleep patterns.

***End each day with the mantra that you have done all that you are willing to do today, and tomorrow is a new day, and you will perform better with rest.***

Here is that term *space* again. Give yourself the permission and space to leave work both physically and mentally. Know that you will perform better if you allow yourself this renewal time. Your brain is like a muscle. It needs time to rest. Chronically thinking about work will only exhaust it.

## **Reflection: Stress-Unbunching and Boundaries**

Think of the last time that you overreacted to a challenge or perceived stressor.

- What triggered you in that moment?
- Did stress-bunching heighten your response?
- How would your reaction have been different if you had not stress-bunched?
- How do you unwind from work now? If you don't currently, how might you?
- How do you transition from work mode to home mode?
- How could you improve this transition?

## **Gratitude**

Gratitude is a great perception shifter and stress interrupter. What you choose to focus on is tightly associated with your attitude, approach, level of optimism, and energy. One of the ways to shift your focus in the moment to something positive is the action of gratitude. While you might be unable to stabilize the environment quickly when challenge hits, equanimous gratitude might help. Being able to quiet your mind when things get tough, untether yourself from reacting, and then shift your focus to the positive gives you room to breathe. A quick way to shift your focus in the moment is the action of gratitude.

Gratitude, and the practice of gratitude, is a way to interrupt a negative thought process. Gratitude is a conscious appreciation of things, events, people, places, etc., and is the act of positive reflection. Gratitude can be practiced as a daily ritual and as an in-the-moment reset. When you get stressed, it's easy to start thinking about all the things that can go wrong. Stress and worry are tightly knotted together, and worry is simply focusing on what "could" go wrong. When we couple stress and worry together, it turns into an escalated trip down the rabbit hole. Stress and worry also distract you from thinking clearly, negatively impacting your health. Worrying more won't prepare you for uncertainty, but calming your mind will. Gratitude helps you to do this by refocusing your mind from what could go wrong to what is going well, and in that moment, you can remember all that is right, all that is good, all that gives life energy, and all that makes you feel at peace.

To clarify, gratitude is not about being thankful for what is not happening, such as "Thank goodness that didn't happen." Instead, gratitude is an act of positively reflecting on what or who is meaningful, helpful, right, just, humorous, joyful, fair, unique, creative etc. For example, stating, "I am grateful for this beautiful sunny day as the light streams into my office," is a statement of gratitude.

Gratitude is not just words; it's a feeling. Pausing to deeply reflect in the moment on something that you are grateful for and feeling deep within your bones and heart is gratitude. Gratitude is a way of affirming to the universe what you want more of, and it is also a way of saying thank you for all that makes your life good. Gratitude can be as simple as "I am grateful for the taste of this beautiful cup of coffee on a rainy day" or as extensive as "I am grateful for my health and feeling well."

Gratitude is a very powerful tool and directly linked to well-being: mind, body, and soul. Gratitude is a mindful endeavor because it focuses our attention in the moment to give thanks. Also, gratitude is not time bound and can involve appreciation for what has happened in the past, what is happening in the present, and the possibilities of the future. Gratitude is a conscious appreciation of what makes life joyful, even the little things.

***Gratitude clears your heart and mind to let kindness and positive possibility enter your realm.***

When we are feeling stressed, we tend to hyperfocus on what is not working in our lives, which can increase our stress levels. The practice of gratitude can help us to shift our focus from what is not working to what is going well in our lives. Researchers Robert Emmons and Michael

McCullough suggest that the practice of gratitude helps to increase our well-being.[3] Focusing on and savouring what is going well in our lives (instead of ruminating on what is not) helps to increase our sense of optimism. There are several ways to practice gratitude, including starting your day with a gratitude journal and reflecting on three things that you are grateful for, or it can be practiced *on the fly* throughout your day. If you start to feel stressed, try pausing to reflect on a few things you are grateful for and feel the gratitude in your body. Take a deep breath.

The practice of gratitude for a leader under stress could be a way to shift the focus from the stressful situation toward more positive solutions and strengths while conjuring the stress-buffering effects of positive emotions in the moment.

### **Gratitude Exercise**

- What are you grateful for? What comes to mind?
- Write down three things you are grateful for.
- Now re-read them, and reflect on how reading them makes you feel. Are you able to feel the gratitude in your bones, and does it soften your heart? Can you feel the positive energy?
- The next time you start to feel stressed, pause to think of three things you are grateful for, and notice how it changes the situation.

# CHAPTER 4

# Finding Calm

- Mindfulness
- Nature As A Psychological Nurturer

***Action is a choice, and reaction can be a choice, too, in the form of a response.***

As a leader, when was the last time you truly felt at peace? Or a sense of pure quiet, deep within your soul? As a leader, it is important to keep filling your psychological reserves bucket to untether yourself from the grip of stress. If your bucket is empty, you will likely get triggered and be less at peace. A leader's skill to remain equanimous or have a calm mind in the face of adversity is their greatest weapon against stress. Being equanimous allows you to *choose* your response while under stress and to remain outside of it, to avoid being overwhelmed by it. Mindfulness and nature can help.

Having the mental power of equanimity does not mean that a leader always has to deploy it or that highly emotional reactions are not allowed. Still, it does mean that a leader can choose how they react and then use equanimity to rebalance. Equanimity is the ability to separate the Self from the moment to hold perspective on both the Self and the situation.

My younger son has the gift of inherent equanimity, and his grounded energy is palpable. He did not inherit this from me or my husband but from my mother and grandmother. When he was born, I remember holding him and feeling his calm and grounded energy. My first thought was, "This kid has amazing energy." His teachers see it, too. He is always the kid seated in the middle of the classroom to ground the classroom, and he is always beside the most difficult child because he grounds them too. Although he is on the quieter side, he holds the energy of the room and everyone in it and knows exactly what roles everyone plays. My son used to also express this talent when playing with his hundreds of toy soldiers. He would position them across our dining room table in perfect order and combat position, knowing everyone's role and understanding that every role was critical to the overall strategy. He would see both the forest and the individual trees of his strategy and co-hold the tension of the differing roles in perfect strategic balance.

While equanimity is a balance and calmness in one's inner spirit and mind, it is also the ability to express this sense of mental order through chaos. An equanimous person does not get sucked into drama, can synthesize information quickly, and is healthily detached from the situation in such a way that they can hold perspective and see the "greater" order of things.

In today's world of impending cyber threats, pandemics, and global warming catastrophes, a leader must remain equanimous amidst the chaos. The more you can maintain your sense of wholeness within chaos, the more your mind can create a strategy *with* perspective. While some are born with a greater tendency for equanimity, it can be cultivated by starting with mindfulness. Mindfulness is about self-awareness in each moment, or the ability to *zone in* to the moment with calm clarity and non-judgement. When you become fully aware of yourself in each moment, you become fully aware of your reactions, feelings, and choices, which frees your mind from distractions and calms your system. You become in control of yourself in a peace-seeking and accepting way.

**Mindfulness**

Mindfulness is essentially about bringing your attention to the present moment. Sometimes the term mindfulness and meditation are used interchangeably. Although they are related, meditation is an activity to help increase mindfulness. In addition to meditation, there are other mindful activities; sometimes, a long quiet walk in nature can be a mindful activity—the smell of the trees, the sound of the birds, and the quiet of the moment can help you to zone in. For me, exercise is a mindful activity, especially a long slow run with my favorite music allows me to tune into my body, live in the notes of the music, and then my mind can stand still. In this space, I am not ruminating on the past, or worried about the future. Instead, I am simply out for a run and in the zone. Swimming in the ocean is another mindfulness experience for me: the turquoise water, the energy of the waves, the feel of the saltwater, and the immersion in nature.

John Kabat-Zinn, a leader in bringing mindful meditation to the Western world, offers that mindfulness helps to increase the ability to uncouple ourselves from situations as a form of self-transcendence.[1] Instead of being in a reactive state and living "in our heads," we can become an observer of situations. In essence, the self becomes uncoupled from the situation—in a healthy way!

A study by Eric Garland, Susan Gaylord, and Barbara Fredrickson found that mindfulness reduces stress levels and enhances the ability to engage in positive reassessments of stressful situations.[2] In addition, Maree Roche, Jarrod Haar, and Fred Luthans studied leaders, managers and entrepreneurs and found that mindfulness helped to reduce anxiety, burnout, and depression.[3] If a leader were able to be more mindful in the moment, they could expand their capacity for untangling themselves from a stressor, create space for more self-regulation, and incorporate less reactive behavior toward stress.

**Types of Mindfulness**

Meditation can be a daunting experiment for people, but it is not the only path to achieving more mindfulness; mindfulness also includes simply attending to the present moment with non-judgement and a heartfelt curiosity. It is more about the experience with the moment. For example, I would argue that downhill skiing is a mindful exercise; the skier has to be one with their body, the equipment, and the snow, and every turn and ski-pole jab has to be intentional. There is no space for mind-wandering. Golf could be another example. Everyone knows that a hot-tempered golfer is going to hit a lot of balls off the green. It's the cool and calm golfers with intense focus that play their best game. Tennis is the same. I really enjoy tennis, when I get too focused on the score I get nervous and it throws my game off. I play my best when I am focused on the ball, the enjoyment of the moment, my physical presence and nothing more. You know when you are engaged in mindfulness when you lose track of time, have a buzzing sense of presentness, and can experience the moment at many levels.

> ***Mindfulness is about zoning into THIS moment and becoming so* present** *that time becomes irrelevant.*

Often, I have clients ask me if watching a movie is mindfulness because they lose track of time. While watching a movie might be relaxing and a nice distraction for the brain, this activity is more about *zoning out*. While zoning out can have a relaxation effect and could be part of a self-care option, it is important to note that this is not a mindful engagement; the movie is not the watcher's reality. I would argue, however, that listening to music can be, but not always, mindful. Sometimes when we listen to a piece of music that deeply moves us, our concentration on that piece is so deep that we can become one with it. We hear every note and lyric and are in a state of full experiential immersion. Art can be mindful as well. Sometimes, when we connect with a piece of art, we experience ourselves in that art or *of* that art, and we are pulled into the moment.

As a leader, mindfulness and mindful practice can help to expand and stretch your mind space. Like any practice, the more you can practice being present, the better you will become at it. Mindfulness can be an intervention in the moment and impact that moment, but it can also have a resonance for future moments.

While it is important that a leader strategize for the future and understand the past, all that anyone really has is the present moment. I point this out only for the purpose of prioritizing your energy to the *here and now*. Focusing on the here and now helps to quiet the noise. What we do today, in this very moment, will impact our future.

**How to Practice Meditation**

The research on the positive health benefits of meditation is massive and undeniable. It can help to improve sleep patterns, lower cortisol levels, and blood pressure, and the list goes on. Meditation doesn't have to be a hugely daunting endeavour. It can be a simple engagement with the moment involving sitting quietly, focusing on your breath, and quieting your mind. If you are currently not a meditator, I would encourage you to explore different methods, styles, and even apps to engage with.

As a former yoga instructor who incorporated meditation into my classes, the one thing that I would offer is to find your own style of meditation and mindfulness—one-size does not fit all. Meditation is a quiet moment with yourself when you can connect to the oneness of this beautiful universe of possibility. Meditation provides a space to simply pause and collect yourself and catch your breath.

If you do not have a current meditation style or technique, I can offer the following as a simple starting point to try daily:

- Set your timer on your smartphone for three mins (to start).
- Sit comfortably, upright, and use your spine and stomach muscles to support you.
- Let your shoulders and jaw relax; think about the muscles in your face relaxing too.
- Take a slow deep breath in so that the air slowly expands the lower part of your lungs, and your belly expands out.
- Hold your breath for a few counts, then exhale *slowly* for a few counts.
- Repeat this breathing technique a few times, then simply sit quietly and notice how you feel, notice your breath.
- Thoughts may come into your mind. Simply let them leave your mind.
- Focus on finding a space in between your thoughts of pure quiet. Sometimes I picture my thoughts as words, and then I try to stretch the space in between my words to find a quiet second.

I suggest starting with three minutes and building it up to five minutes. It's about slowing down your breath, slowing down your thoughts, relaxing your muscles, and feeling your presence in THIS moment. Perhaps try meditating before your next stressful or demanding meeting to see if you can notice its impact.

**Worry isn't realty, but this moment is.**

## Nature

As a leader under stress, it is likely that you are spending long hours in boardrooms, on the computer, in offices, and travelling, while not spending enough time in nature. Immersion into nature not only feels good, but it also helps to calm the mind, re-energizes the spirit, and positively impacts your well-being. Being in nature is part of our deep genetic makeup. It is a mindful activity that sparks areas of our brain, including curiosity and wonder. Nature also takes you out of your office and physically immerses you in a space full of color, natural light, and sensory stimulation, all while pulling your mind away from work. Nature can provide a place for mind renewal.

Being in nature is shown to decrease the stress reaction, improve mood, lower cortisol, increase immune systems, increase vitality, lower heart rate, and increase cognitive performance.[4] Not only can nature improve well-being, it can also buffer against the negative impacts of stress, both physiologically and psychologically.

Nature is a natural nurturer for stress resiliency and recovery. As leaders are constrained by long working days, multiple distractions, and few breaks from their computers and smartphones, there is little personal time left to spend renewing in nature. Yet, spending time in nature can improve our ability to concentrate by allowing our attention to rest and renew.[5]

Mindfulness, especially when coupled with nature, is a way to calm your mind. Equanimity requires mindfulness. Being present in the moment and removing mental distractions allows you to synthesize the information around you and inside of you. Equanimity is about taking a moment to process before reacting, and mindfulness stretches your capacity to pause. Nature supports both of these capacities.

**The Feeling of Mindfulness**

Mindfulness is how you experience the moment. It is a feeling and sensing. When you are being mindful in the moment you are awake, alert, engaged, aware, and relaxed simultaneously. Equanimity is mindfulness, but it also adds the ability to be completely aware of your thoughts and thinking to the moment and engage in action in a relaxed awareness of being, doing, and thinking.

Cultivating more mindfulness in your life by engaging in nature, meditation, and flow (through things you are curious and interested in) will help to cultivate more equanimity in your life. Make time for your interests, curiosity projects, favourite sports, favourite past-times, and hobbies because it will help to expand your ability to be present and aware, and it feels good.

The more time you spend away from your interests, the longer the path back, and you start to forget what sparks you. In reality, I realize that time is limited, but knowing that spending even a little time each day on a passion project, reading an article of interest, or whatever it is that feels like YOU, is time invested in your superpower of equanimity. Our brains get crowded by so many "I should" statements that we start to lose sight of the "I am, and I enjoy" statements. Take time with yourself in an endeavor that sparks you and helps you to enter flow.

## Reflection on Mindfulness

- When was the last time you felt completely present?
- What is your go-to activity to "gather" yourself?
- What makes you pause in the present?
- How do you feel in nature? How does it impact your energy levels?
- Do you get enough time in nature?
- Think back to when you were young. How did being in nature make you feel?

## Activity This Week: Getting back to Nature

- Do something in nature this week, even if it's a quick walk to a local park. Notice the trees, the sky, the birds, etc. Notice how it makes your mind and body feel.
- For as little as twenty minutes, engage in something that you are curious about or simply love doing.

# CHAPTER 5

# Perspective

- Growth Mindset
- SISU

*"The greatest discovery of any generation is that a human can alter his life by altering his attitude." –William James, philosopher and psychologist.*

How we engage with the world and persevere relies on our attitude. I would argue that attitude is how we carry ourselves, mindset is the choice we make in how to carry ourselves, and perspective is what helps to shape our mindset. Persepctive, mindset, attitude.

Below this iceberg of attitude is a myriad of under-the-surface feelings, experiences, and emotions such as optimism, confidence, self-efficacy, cultural experiences, aptitude, fears, hopes, and dreams. Regardless of what is under the surface, attitude is still a conscious choice. For example, even when afraid, we can still choose to be brave.

Awareness is the first step, and the second step is consciously choosing to adjust, if necessary. Attitude is part of a complex feedback system because choosing a positive or constructive attitude will impact how we engage with the world, increasing our chances of a positive outcome, which then feeds back into our choices for the future. In a sense, there is nothing to lose in adopting a positive attitude, mindset, and perspective. A positive attitude has nothing to do with naivety because you can have a positive attitude while also being aware of potential challenges.

**Sisu**

My father's entire side of the family is Finnish. In Finnish culture, there is an expression that relates to mindset and attitude called Sisu. Sisu loosely translates to mean grit, perseverance, courage, and will at a deep cellular level. I remember my Finnish grandmother using the word when she referred to someone who had a strong presence and seemed empowered by a greater force. Someone with Sisu doesn't get rocked easily, is the opposite of a fragile spirit, and tends to lead their life with courage and authenticity. I would argue that someone with Sisu also has the power of equanimity because they are able to rise above the distractions and comparisons to focus on the task.

My Finnish grandmother would describe my eldest son, who was only a toddler then, as having a lot of Sisu. When he was born, my first thought was, "This boy is fierce." Not in an aggressive way, but his energy is strong and present. Today as a young adult, he is a gentle-hearted person but strong as an ox, and when he enters a room, you know it. He has a fierce spirit; when my son decides on something, you know he will do it, period, end of story. Raising a son who has a lot of Sisu has been an absolute privilege, but I struggled for a while as I tried to keep up with him until I realized that it was just about getting out of his way. I had to find the balance of wanting to protect him, but allowing him his autonomy…I am still working on it! Autonomy to a person with a high degree of Sisu is essential, and trying to constrain them is counterproductive.

I would add to the definition of Sisu that it is a forward-moving force that doesn't concern itself with mediocracy because it is too busy setting its sights on the task. Someone with Sisu doesn't get distracted by comparison or worry about what others might think. Someone with Sisu sets their own path and is in fearless pursuit of their dreams.

Although Sisu can be a natural tendency, it can also be cultivated. Sisu is about mentally getting out of your own way. Sisu uses clarity, fortitude, and authenticity as its guiding force, leaving little room for the distractions of worry and fear; the same goes for equanimity. Sisu starts with knowing your strengths and working *with them* instead of against them, which enables you to be self-anchored. Think of trying to paddle upstream all of the time against something you are not. It is exhausting. Sisu is about using the power of energy and working with the forces to accelerate your journey.

Sisu is also the follow-through after you have gained your clarity through equanimity. Sisu, in equanimity, is about shifting your energy from focusing on *who you are not* to *who you are* in a mindfulness-to-the-moment pursuit. Sisu doesn't mean that you don't fail, but it does mean that if you don't succeed, you immediately "right" yourself like a sailboat and carry on the voyage.

> ***What you are curious about is an indicator of the strength you are developing.***

Understanding your strengths start with self-awareness, and self-awareness is developed through reflection, curiosity, and feedback. How do others see you? How would others describe you? How would you describe yourself? Never be afraid of feedback, and always seek it from trusted sources. This reflective information is a gift. Make it your mission to be clear on what is natural to you and what your competitive advantage is. Coaching is a great place to develop more self-awareness and clarity on your strengths.

Self-awareness of your strengths is also about understanding which strength may go into overdrive while under stress. Personally, I am a natural organizer; I can find a process and develop logistics from chaos, in fact, I enjoy it. Under stress, especially derived from a tight deadline, I have to be careful with this strength because I can become too rigid by applying too much process, which can stifle creativity. When I am in overdrive with my organizational skills I can feel it (at least when I am being self-aware!). I can feel the rigidity of this strength in over-drive; my communication becomes slightly curt, I create task lists upon task lists, and I feel rushed. If I am being self-aware, I work on pausing, breathing, relaxing my shoulders, going for a walk, and slowing down. In fact,

I keep a small wooden turtle by my computer as a symbol and visual reminder to slow down.

***Knowing who you are unleashes the bounds that hold you to all that you are not.***

Let's pause for a moment for a personal reflection.

### **Reflection: A Few of Your Strengths**.

- List five examples of what you feel are your top strengths and character attributes.
- List five examples of what you feel others would say are your top strengths.
- Ask someone you trust to tell you what they feel are your top strengths.
- As a kid, what were a few of your natural strengths? Which role did you play in the playground?
- What new strengths have you developed as an adult?
- What strengths would you like to improve?
- Who is a role model for you, and what are their strengths?
- What are you most curious about? Why?
- Under stress, which strength do you deploy the most? Which are most helpful?
- Under stress, which strength can go into overdrive if you don't moderate it?

**Equanimity, Stress, and a Sisu Mindset**

Part of the ability to untangle yourself from stress begins with your mindset, or in other words, how your approach the situation. Starting with the groundbreaking work of psychologist Dr. Carol Dweck in *fixed* and *growth* mindset[1] (she has helpful lectures available online), a fixed mindset or threat mindset carries a higher stress level and a desire to avoid the situation, whereas a growth mindset, or a challenge mindset, is an open and approach stance to a situation. A growth mindset enables you to lead with an "Even if I don't have the answers now, I will figure it out." It helps you dig into your inner resources and seek help when needed. In essence, our mindset matters to our performance.

Between the perception of the stressor and your reaction to it, there is an assessment space that is influenced by such things as beliefs, triggers, biases, mindsets, etc. How a leader becomes aware of *that space* and develops *that space* as an antecedent to a stress reaction involves self-awareness, mindset awareness and equanimity.

> *Positive reframing is about resetting your viewpoint to look at things with a learning mindset.*

Similar to the glass half empty or half full, perspective and mindset are critical in how an individual sees the world and reacts. Dweck's research into a *fixed* or *growth* mindset has shown that how we approach a task from the outset matters to the possibility of a successful performance.[2] A fixed mindset may lead you to say, "I can't do this task. It seems too hard," which is a closed and negative energy, whereas a growth mindset would change this statement to "I don't know how to do this task now, but I've figured other things out in the past, so I'll give it a good try," which keeps the energy open to possibility.

During times of uncertainty, a leader who approaches a challenge with a growth mindset will be more apt to try new things, seek feedback, ask for help, and take risks. In addition, if a leader approaches a challenge with a growth mindset, they will engage with a challenge, keep an open mind, lead with a sense of faith in their competency, and not be afraid to fail.

Even when things get tough, choose optimism and the possibility of growth in the moment.

***A growth mindset is optimism in action.***

You can have fixed mindsets for some tasks and growth ones for others. For example, I may feel competent with math and approach math with a growth mindset, "I can figure math out" attitude, while at the same time have a fixed mindset with science and think, "Science is too hard for me. It's not my thing." A growth mindset positions you into an optimistic *approach* mode where you become more open to learning and feedback. But a fixed mindset positions you into an *avoidant* stance in which you are threatened.

A fixed mindset is an energy drain that blocks possibility, whereas a growth mindset allows for exploration and possibility and is *energy-charged* with optimism. Having a growth mindset doesn't mean that you will succeed at everything you try, but it does open the pathway to potential and learning. Sisu requires a growth mindset to optimistically engage in a challenge without being afraid to fail. Equanimity can help you to pause before you choose your mindset wisely.

**Optimism**

Optimism is the positive perspective an individual has for their future. Research suggests that remaining optimistic through times of stress can conjure more effective "approach" coping behaviors and well-being, in essence, people with optimism are more inclined to lean into finding solutions when things get tough.[3] Feeling good about the future in times of stability is easier than holding a positive expectation during times of uncertainty. It is important to remember that optimism is about *expectation,* not *certainty,* and is a proactive sense of faith that all will be well. A leader's ability to remain optimistic in times of uncertainty is helpful in remaining hopeful and maintaining a positive mindset.

> ***Optimism is about expectation, not about certainty.***

Not only will optimism help you to positively engage in a challenge, but it is also better for your health! Groundbreaking research by Suzanne Segerstrom and Sandra Sephton indicates that optimism could be positively correlated with immunity, a critical factor in staying healthy while under stress when cortisol levels increase inflammation.[4]

While some people naturally are more optimistic, it should be noted that optimism is still a choice, and it starts with awareness of the Self. Are you a naturally optimistic person? If so, why are you optimistic, and how did you learn to be? If not, why not? Optimism is not Pollyannaism or an excessive and slightly blind, and unrealistic look at the future. Instead, it is a sense of *hopefulness in action* about the future. Uncertainty, while challenging, does not always align with bad. It can be a positive chance for change and growth too.

What is your tendency for a mindset? And optimism?

## **Let's pause for a moment of personal reflection:**

- Do you tend to be optimistic or pessimistic?
- Is your level of optimism somewhat fragile? If so, why?
- What helps you to feel optimistic?
- With which tasks do you take risks? With which tasks do you play it safe?
- Think of a leader you admire. Which mindset do they have, fixed or growth?
- Which tasks would you like to switch from a fixed to a growth mindset? Why?
- With which tasks from your past have you had a growth mindset, and how did it help you?

# CHAPTER 6

# Choosing Happiness

- Emotions and Equanimity
- Personal Mantras

*Finnish proverb: "ei se pelaa joka pelkää"*

**Translation: "that who fears won't play"**

Staying stuck in the weeds as a leader happens when you have become accustomed to focusing on problems; getting out of the weeds is when you become focused on finding solutions. Our brains are hardwired to be vigilant as a survival mechanism, but this vigilance sometimes guides us astray from being able to think strategically. This tendency can lead you to focus on problems and negative emotions as a form of protection. As a counter to this vigilance, equanimity can help you to assess the perceived threat in tandem with discovering the opportunities.

The next time that you are in a boardroom or on a video call with collective voices focusing on what *can't be* done or what is not going well be sure to ask, "What are we able to do?" or "In spite of all this, what is going well? Tell me one thing." There is power in choosing the positive. Even in the heart of a storm, there is something positive; what you see and experience depends on what you choose to focus on.

I am not suggesting by any means to neglect the challenges you need to address, but what I am saying is to also not neglect the positive in times of crisis or everyday life. It's easy to fall into the trap of putting out fires and leaving no time to strategize. Strategy is where "fire prevention" happens.

**Fear-Focused**

As our brains are wired for vigilance, we can become too fear-focused. Often, fear is simply worry, and worry is a negative assumption or perception of our reality. If we can change our perception, we can change our emotion of fear, which will impact our behavior and performance. Part of changing our perception is changing what we choose to focus on.

Fear is about choosing to focus on what could go wrong, whereas hope and preparation are about focusing our efforts on what *can* be done, what is possible, and what could be within our control. Essentially, choosing to shift your focus from fear to possibility will help you get to the work of supporting things going right.

> ***Choosing possibility will help you give the situation a chance to go well.***

**Leader Focus**

If you have taken a psychology course, you may have heard the term *locus of control*.[1] An *internal* locus of control occurs when an individual feels that their actions matter to the outcome and relates to a sense of personal empowerment. When facing uncertainty, a leader needs to believe that they have the capacity to *figure it out* and the ability to impact the outcome. In contrast, an *external* locus of control occurs when an individual feels that their choice is outside of their control and they are not empowered by their actions and decisions.

There are many things and situations outside of our control, but what you choose to focus on is always owned by you. Even when you feel as though your *back is up against the wall*, shifting your mind, and being conscious of the empowerment of choice, are helpful in grounding yourself. What you choose to focus on is tightly associated with your attitude, approach, level of optimism, energy, and performance. It is very draining to believe everything is out of your control; powerlessness is debilitating.

The next time you face a challenge or crisis as a leader, pause with your power of equanimity to ask yourself: what is outside of my control, and what is within my control? Pausing to process and decipher points of control helps you to shift your focus to possibility and to target your energy where it could have an impact. Using the power of equanimity, when faced with a challenge, can broaden your view on a situation, depersonalize it, and turn your focus inward to what is within your control.

**Positive Emotions**

In addition to shifting your focus to what is within your control, focusing on positive emotions can also help to refocus your energy from negativity to possibility. Happiness breeds more happiness. While negative emotions and stress are a part of life, consciously and intentionally seeking more positive emotions can enhance your well-being and performance.

Seeking joyful activities can sometimes be a lost art when things get busy. Too often, I hear leaders say, "I have no time for XYZ" or "I'll do that (fun thing) when I am on holiday." Even when things are busy, incorporating activities that bring you joy is crucial for your health and performance. Research suggests that positive emotions help you think better; renowned professor and psychology scholar Barbara Fredrickson found that positive emotions impact perception because when an individual is experiencing a positive emotion, their cognitive capacity broadens, enabling them to take in more contextual information.[2] This broader thinking ability is tied to synthesizing information better and faster and working through the mire of complexity.

For example, let's take fictious Negative Ned. Negative Ned is great at spotting problems and identifying what can go wrong on a deal. When Ned enters a room, you can feel the energy deflate, and you can notice the creativity in the conversation dwindle. Although Ned might be correct about potholes in the road, his mood and energy leave little space for creative thinking. Ned expresses the hypervigilant side in all of us, and his comments make us forget the possibility; instead, his tunnelled vision is contagious to the team, in almost a groupthink.

On the contrary, you likely know a Positive Pat (fictious). Pat arrives at meetings with a smile and an aura of optimism. Pat, in times of challenge, is the one who rolls up his sleeves and gets to work by asking questions and working to find a solution. When he enters the room, the energy shifts from worry to action. Pat helps the room's energy to spin from "What can go wrong?" to "What can we do?"

It's easy to focus on negative emotions because they are of high potency and feel safe and familiar. On the contrary, positive emotions, while equally potent feel more vulnerable such as optimism; it takes courage to be optimistic. Because of our vigilant survival brains, it feels easier and safer to be negative and close to worry, so it takes conscious recalibration to choose positive emotions and to seek activities that bring happiness.

> ***Approaching life with an optimistic and happy attitude actually feels scarier and more vulnerable because you have a sense of more to lose.***

## Fear of Happiness?

Loss aversion theory suggests that people make choices in order to *not lose* what they have. It acts as a bias or lens in decision-making. Loss aversion theory suggests that we act to protect what we already have. This is similar to making decisions (or not) based on fear and worry because they are decisions rooted in avoiding loss.

While there is a time and place for making decisions based on fear and avoiding loss, I would also argue that nothing great was ever discovered or developed rooted in fear. Growth and expansion take the positive emotion of optimism, and positive energy to support new initiatives.

Positive emotions not only aid you in performing better while under stress, but they are also good for your overall well-being and help you to recover better from stress. As a leader, imagine how cultivating more positive emotions can impact your mood and positively infect the mood of others around you! Positive emotions help to clear the distractions of worry and open the lens or aperture for possibility, essentially, all that could go well. The next time you feel your emotions head "south" and become fear-based, try to do something to interrupt it, knowing that positive emotions are more helpful. Seek joy, choose happiness, remember to practice gratitude, compliment someone, lighten your heart, and even wear something colourful or be sure to listen to great music on the way to work.

### **Reflection: Positive Emotion**

- What three things bring you joy?
- What makes you deeply laugh?
- What helps you to feel optimistic and puts you in an optimistic mindset?
- What activity could you add to your life to bring you more joy and light-heartedness?

It is also important to remember that positive emotions have a resonance, and the more you nurture them, the more they will grow. Being happy is a skill, a positive habit, and a daily choice. Even when the wind is blowing in your face, smile.

> ***Optimism and positive emotions invite solutions.***

**Emotions and Equanimity**

Becoming more aware of your emotions and mood is supported by becoming more equanimous. Perception and thoughts drive behavior, so becoming aware of unnecessary negative thinking, worry, and fear will directly impact your mood. Be mindful of your thinking, be mindful of your mood, and be mindful of your choices and actions. In a state of equanimity, you can become more conscious of your ability to choose happier thoughts and responses simply by becoming more aware of your lens.

**Personal Mantras**

On the topic of positive emotions, I wanted to mention the concept of creating a personal mantra as an interrupter to negative thinking. A personal mantra is a quick and easy way to intentionally refocus your attention and reset when you need to. Developing a personal mantra involves reflecting on what you are grateful for, what is meaningful to you, and what your greatest strengths are.

Recalling your mantra when things get difficult can help to pull you into the realm of positive emotions.

An important aspect of a personal mantra is that it has to be authentic to be effective. A personal mantra is a simple statement that you keep close to your heart and soul. Mantras can be profound, metaphorical, inspirational, grounding, simple, etc.—whatever you need them to be. It's your choice.

## **Reflection: Creating a Mantra**

- Do you have a current mantra?
- What do you say to yourself when things get tough?
- What virtues and values come to the forefront when faced with a lot of stress?
- What is one of your favorite inspirational lines from a book, song, movie, or person?
- What could you say to yourself to refocus?

## **Activity This Week: Practising your Mantra**

After writing a mantra, or a few of them, put them into practice this week. When you start to feel a little stress creeping in or your mood turning negative, try interrupting it with your mantra. Notice how (if) it changes the moment and your perspective. Try different ones to see which one is more *charged* for you.

# CHAPTER 7

# Mind Agility

- Biases & Thinking Errors
- Resilience

> *"Whatever is flexible and flowing will tend to grow; whatever is rigid and blocked will wither and die."* –Tao Te Ching

Expect the unexpected has become the new norm, leaving leaders with complex challenges and no precedented protocols. There is no rule book to address the new ways of doing things. That is why inner wisdom is a key success skill. When there isn't anything to guide you, you (and your team) have to figure out how to create your own path—pioneers of the new frontier.

While leaders may not necessarily be seasoned in the new challenges, they can be experienced in navigating uncertainty through cultivated personal resilience and by adopting an agile way. Agility is about going with the flow while still understanding the currents. Similar to how a skinny palm tree can withstand hurricane force by bending with the wind, a leader can withstand the storms of change by being flexible.

Before any great change or growth, there is a tension of letting go of the old way of doing things and breaking through to the new. Growing pains are not only a metaphorical experience but also a biological one. It can hurt to grow, and it can hurt to change sometimes. However, the more flexible (especially in your perspective and mind) you are to accept and welcome the growth process, the less "hurt" you will have to endure because you will bend with the force of change instead of fight against it.

If something (or someone) is too rigid to withstand the forces of growth, they could break with the tension because growth requires some *give*. Think of a simple analogy of the chicken cracking out of the shell or an adult tooth breaking through a child's gum—tension and discomfort associated with a forward energy.

There can also be an emotional 'hurt' side to growth, for example, a parent watching their child leave for university or drive away with their newly acquired driver's license; growth and discomfort are a shared comradery, like yin and yang. Expectations and perspectives can help with this tension and discomfort. When you expect change to be easy, you will likely be in for a surprise, but if you expect the tension associated with growth, then it's part of your planning and foresight.

> ***As change happens, and as you overcome challenges, you grow.***

I remember during the Adult Development module of my doctoral studies, I was having an opinionated discussion about the necessity and reality of growth tension with my professor; I used to argue that growth *can* happen without tension. I would wonder, Why does there have to be a sense of tension to resolve in order to grow? However, I began to reflect that it was harder and harder to find an example of real growth without some kind of tension, adversity, or discomfort. The only exceptions that I could conjure were epiphanies or AHA moments, but it's arguable that there could also be tension preceding those experiences as well.

As I reflected, I realized all my true growth moments required some sort of tension, including getting fit for a run, giving birth to my sons, working hard for my doctoral studies, leaving an unhealthy relationship behind, and delivering a keynote; there was hurt and hardship in all of these growing experiences. I began to understand that if I could help my clients (and myself) change the perspective and expectation surrounding growing pains from one of frustration to acknowledgement that positive change was afoot, then it might help lessen its impact. After all, achieving something after hard work feels way better than achieving something by mere luck. Meaningful change.

Accepting the situation for what it is, is half the battle. Denial will only lead to more denial, whereas facing a challenge or area in need of change head-on takes courage and starts the growth process, as difficult as it might be.

**Equanimity and Change Tension**

Approaching change, and the pains that come with it, with an approach stance is energizing to the growth itself. Equanimity resides here by helping us become clearly aware of what is going "on" during the change and by increasing our ability to acknowledge our thinking and attitudes during the process, including identifying any self-inflicted resistors. It is important to assess our mindset when facing a new challenge to ensure that it is not a preprogrammed bias getting in our way and causing resistance. If you feel yourself resisting to change, use equanimity to pause and become aware of "why?" you are thinking and feeling th resistance. Also remember to be compassionate with yourself during change and let go of the notion that you need to be an expert, instead focus on being a good learner. Be sure to not weigh yourself down by unnecessary self-doubt based on falsely imagined beliefs and expectations. Being a leader does not require being an expert, the only expert you need to be as a leader is an expert learner.

> ***Go easy on yourself during change, don't pressure yourself to be an expert, but be an expert learner. Eyes, ears, mind and heart wide open.***

Greater equanimity can assist in enabling you to pause to check in with how you think and feel and help you assess the situation less critically. We tend to be our own worst critic. When you can become more aware of this inner resistance, you are more likely to be able to maneuvre around it, or shed it altogether! Your cognitive load becomes less as you shed unnecessary bad habits in thinking, freeing up more mind-space to embrace change for what it is.

> *Learning is a flexible, agile, and adaptive practice. Learning is a growing and expanding endeavour.*

Take a few moments to reflect on any resistors in your learning habits and thinking habits.

## **Personal Reflection:**

- Think of the last great moment of growth in your life. What tension or hurt came before it? How did it help your growth?
- Do you put unnecessary pressure on yourself to be an expert, or do you focus on being a great learner?

## **Resiliency**

Resiliency is a two-fold concept. It encompasses being agile in the moment and recovering quickly or *righting oneself* after a challenging moment. I always like to think of a sailing metaphor with respect to resiliency. The wind can be howling against the sail, and the captain has to hold the wind tension in the sail with the right amount of counter tension to contain the energy but also needs to loosen the sails when needed—it's a constant adjustment and an evolving process of awareness. If the wind gets so strong, the sailboat is designed (hopefully) with its heavy keel to right itself. So it has a built-in system to be resilient.

Resiliency is, perhaps, more inherent in some people based on a plethora of factors such as learned behaviors, culture, etc., but like most other traits, resiliency can be cultivated. Renowned positive psychology researchers Kate Hefferon and Ilona Boniwell identified six common traits of resilient individuals: ability to reframe; high level of positive emotions; regular participation in physical activity; a trusted social support system; the use of personal strengths; and optimism.[1] Each of these common traits of resiliency can grow through intentional activities.

The growth of your personal resiliency doesn't depend on just one action but instead is a conscious action to increase your well-being and equanimity, too. For example:

- Being physically fit feeds into your psychological resiliency, especially when doing exercise in nature, for the added boost.
- Seeking positive emotions is critical; happiness breeds happiness, which fuels increases in energy and resources.
- Having healthy and supportive friends and family is also part of a resilience plan—being able to talk things out, feel listened to, and being a good friend to others.
- Knowing what your strengths are and how to deploy them, but also your areas in need of development.

**Of the traits of resiliency, how would you score on a scale of one to ten (ten being great)?**

- Ability to positively reframe a situation in the moment
- Relationships and support
- Physical fitness

- Optimism
- Positive emotions (daily)
- Awareness of your strengths and use of them

**Reflection:**

- What was your highest score? What was your lowest score? Why?
- What could you start, stop and continue to increase your resiliency?

**Resiliency and Agility**

The trick and the talent of equanimity is being aware *in the moment* of the action and reaction so that you can make adjustments. Equanimity helps to anchor your thinking to the present moment, enabling you to return to your center when you need to. This is not to say that emotions are not allowed, but it's about processing emotions, regulating them, and expressing only the emotions that you want (and need) to. Essentially, responding rather than reacting.

Equanimity helps to increase resiliency because it aids with an increase in self-awareness and the ability to hold perspective while also changing course if needed. In essence, becoming more cognitively supple or agile while also being able to bounce back after a negative event.

**Agility and Stress**

Navigating through stress is about moving and flowing with life energy instead of against the current. Think of the concept of paddling upstream against the force of the moving water as opposed to loosening the oars, while maintaining control, and then using the current to cruise downstream with the water. Being flexible is about letting go a bit, not losing control of the boat, and not trying to control energy that can't be controlled. Agility is about trusting yourself to move through change without all of the answers.

It is stressful and exhausting to fight change. Letting go a little frees up energy and helps you to move with the change, as opposed to against it, by being cognitively supple.

As with every great athlete, part of the training is flexibility. The more flexible the athlete, and in the right way (over-flexibility can lead to injury too), the less likely the injury and the greater the ability to perform. Using the athletic analogy, the athlete also must be strong too. Both strength and flexibility require training and a sustained commitment to practice. Similarly, being agile and flexible as a leader and building your strengths takes training and practice too.

> ***"The measure of intelligence is the ability to change." –Albert Einstein***

Let's take a close look at fictious Fixed Finley. You likely know someone just like him. Finley is very good at making decisions and setting the path forward. Finley seems to know what she is doing most of the time, but she never really polls the team for their buy-in ideas, nor does she ask a lot of questions or opinions of others.

Finley seems to be constantly in task mode, doesn't like to engage in "small talk," and gets impatient with extensive group discussions. While you appreciate Finley's initiative, sometimes you can find her overbearing, and sometimes around her, you feel like you can't think or express an opinion because you will get in her way. Finley likes to rush and has, in the past, rushed to make a decision that was not necessarily the right one. Then the team had to backtrack to fix something. Finley doesn't seem to understand the importance of taking time at the outset to think more strategically and critically or to be able to change course when necessary. Finley's style can be militaristic, and it stifles creativity at times, in spite of her good intentions of getting the job done.

Do you know a Fixed Finley? Have you been a Finley before? Let's face it, we all can become a Fixed Finley when we feel the constraint of time pressures or feel unsure. Sometimes any action feels better than no action, and time can feel like a luxury. However, resiliency and agility are about not rushing to fix something but instead being flexible in finding new insights and adjusting to meet new challenges. Sometimes the old ways of doing things work, but sometimes they don't, and it's important to use equanimity to pause and assess the situation fully. And then, it is critical to ask the team wholeheartedly for their input. Listening and equanimity go hand in hand.

### **Reflection: Agility**

- What are you flexible about? What are you not flexible about?

- Would people, in general, describe you as flexible and agile? If so why? If not, why?
- What would you like to become more agile with?
- What will it take to be more agile in this area of your life?
- What are you currently paddling upstream against? What would happen if you let go of the oars a bit?
- Who do you admire most? Are they a flexible person?

## **Activity for the Week: Become more Agile**

- Notice this week when you go into fast-fixer mode. Pause and ask yourself why you defaulted here.
- Notice this week when you are being flexible and able to "go with the flow." Ask yourself, "What factors need to be in place for me to feel fluid and go with the flow or let go a bit?" and "What is it about this situation that is different from a situation in which I feel rigid?"
- Ask more questions and listen more to your team this week, and see what happens. Examples of questions that entice more listening:

  - "Huh, tell me more about your thinking on that idea?"
  - "I am curious, what's behind your thinking on this one? What led you to this?"
  - "What does your gut say?"

- "If we could have one perfect fix, what would it look like?"
- "What do you think the biggest resistor is?"
- "What does the quick fix on this look like, and what does the long-term, more sustained fix look like?... are they the same?"
- "What do you think we are missing?"
- "What's the fly on the wall thinking and wanting to say?

# CHAPTER 8

# How to Befriend Change

- Tolerance for Ambiguity

Let's face it; change is challenging. This is part of the tension of growth. The superpower of equanimity can help ease the tension of change by helping you to:

- uncouple from what doesn't need to be personalized
- contain the challenge to what it is and no more
- hold a view on the horizon, and remember that it is temporary
- be your best Self in the face of adversity
- remain in a growth mindset, sparked with optimism

Equanimity affords you the opportunity to positively engage with the challenge of change instead of avoiding it. The amount of equanimity you can conjure during change will help make it smoother and less tangled with unnecessaries.

The challenge of change has a knack of sometimes feeling overwhelming, igniting our anxieties, and then triggering our vigilant tendencies, which can lead to resistance. This resistance can either lead to rushing to find a solution to relieve the tension or avoiding it altogether. When we rush into task mode to solve the challenge, we only "plug the hole" or try to "put a Band-Aid" on to make it go away instead of looking at the bigger picture and exploring it in its entirety. A quick-fixer task mode is *management,* not leadership. Leadership mode is slowing down the process (no matter how painful) to look at the whole picture, and collect all of the voices, ideas, and data.

This reminds me of my uncle, who is a retired airline captain. My uncle would never just fly the plane. Instead, he would fly the people, fly the aircraft, fly the wind, etc. One of his regular practices was to get outside of the cockpit preflight for a walk around the airplane to look at its entirety. As the captain, he appreciated the bigger picture of the aircraft's integrity and the importance of using all of his senses to ensure all was well. He understood that simply sitting in the captain's chair only gave him a limited view. The other thing about my uncle is that I have never seen him rush. Everything is done with methodical precision. This methodical precision is a kind of equanimity or the ability to remain collected under pressure, consider all facets at once, and make calculated and synthesized decisions on the fly.

**Tolerance for Ambiguity**

Leaning into tackling issues requires you to be in the zone, and *in the process*, as opposed to worrying about the outcome. If you were to engage with a challenge with a fixed mindset and presumption that you needed to already be an expert, your stress level would rise, and your cognitive abilities would narrow. Staying open and in a learning-growth-Sisu mindset helps to expand your tolerance for ambiguity. Tolerance for ambiguity, or comfort level with the unknown, is about being okay with not knowing all of the answers from the outset and trusting yourself to figure it out as you go. There is an element of letting go that accompanies an increased tolerance for ambiguity and being comfortable with not knowing the destination while being mindfully focused on the NOW.

> ***Leaders need only to be experts at learning.***

Tolerance for ambiguity is on a continuum; some things make you more uncomfortable than others, and some days you might be better at it than others. Getting to the root of what helps you to be more *okay* with change, and then doing more of it, as a proactive measure when faced with the unknown, is part of expanding your tolerance. It's a conscious effort.

Mindset also matters. A fixed mindset lends itself to a low tolerance for uncertainty, and a growth mindset opens your mind. Mindfulness helps too. Simply being present in the process as it unfolds while trusting your strengths helps to expand your tolerance for the lack of a "clear-cut solution". In essence, it's about simply trusting in yourself and approaching each task steeped in your personal capabilities, along with the curiosity and enjoyment of doing the work. This is where equanimity comes into play. Equanimity pulls you into the moment in a balanced and detached way so that you can do a full walkabout of the challenge with an openness to figure it out, identify any internal resistors, and ease into the challenge with a "figure it out" attitude.

Remember to slow down the process when faced with the challenge of change, do a walkabout of your "aircraft," engage with all of your senses, see the big picture, and look for the fine detail.

### **Reflection: Tolerance for Ambiguity**

Take a moment to reflect on the following:

- How is your general tolerance for ambiguity? Does change and uncertainty make you uncomfortable or excite you?
- Now think of your differing tolerance for ambiguity. Which situations are better at it? Which situations and topics are less comfortable?
- Think of a past situation when you were able to go with the flow. What was it about that particular situation that helped?

While tolerance for ambiguity is contextual, it can also be tied to inherent tendencies to some degree. Some people (leaders) naturally want to apply process and order to chaos as an immediate form of action, while others are quite comfortable sitting with chaos. Everyone has a different working style. My default tendency, especially while under stress, is to organize and apply the process quickly. I find comfort in having a plan, meeting deadlines in an orderly fashion, and I am much less comfortable going with the flow if there is a task to complete. As I mentioned previously, while this tendency can be a strength, in overdrive, it is a challenge of mine. So being armed with this self-awareness, I work on trying to pause when I *physically* feel the sensation to hit the "go mode." The slower my reaction time to more robustly assess the information, the quicker I can target the real issue that needs my attention.

**The Tension of Change**

Tension during changes exists. Very seldom does change or challenge happen without some sort of chamber where it feels like things are getting worse rather than improving. I have heard that in homeopathic medicine, this is called a healing crisis. I like to think of this period of growth and change as the bridge between point A to point B. The metaphor of a bridge expresses the tension between two points. If there was no tension, there would be no bridge. Otherwise, it would be too weak and floppy to sustain the weight of the passengers traversing it.

However, many times when change does *not* happen, it is a result of this tension becoming so intense that it will cause a person to default back to point A or choose another path to avoid it. The expression "Better the devil you know than the devil you don't" comes to mind. Rationalizing what is causing us some angst is important to remain critically reflective in decision-making to ensure that we are not simply choosing the easier path but not the right one.

*Sameness is comforting, but sameness doesn't mean growth.*

Growth requires tension. Being okay with the tension of change takes practice and awareness. Simply understanding that change is hard and that change feels uncomfortable helps to form an expectancy around the unexpected. For example, shift your mind dialogue to "This discomfort I feel is simply the tension before the growth that will happen. It's a good sign."

**I am expecting growth, but I am equally expecting discomfort before the growth: growing *pains!***

I am not suggesting ignoring signs and feelings that the current path to resolve the challenge or change is incorrect. Gut instinct plays a role in helping to identify if the mild angst you feel is simply because it's hard or wrong. This is why it is important to be self-aware in discerning feelings of resistance. Easier said than done, I know. Use your equanimity here to really look *hard* and *broad* at the situation, ensure that it aligns with your values, and ask if it will lead to growth for all.

*True growth is about the ability to release a moment from what it was to invite the new moment it will become.*

*Change is messy, change is uncomfortable, but change is also exciting.*

Becoming comfortable with change is part of being a leader, and cultivating your ability to be mindful, metacognitive, and equanimous is helpful to expanding your invitation of change. While there are external challenges that you have no control over, you can channel your thoughts about the situation. I am reminded of a Finnish proverb that suggests, "The forest will answer in the way in which it was called." Your future will be shaped by your thoughts today. Choose wisely. Embrace change with open arms. Be okay with the tension of change. Be kind to yourself, the change, and the moment.

**Self-Compassion**

It is hard to reflect on the tolerance for ambiguity and the tension of change without reflecting on the importance of self-compassion. Being okay with the messiness of change also means being okay with your faults (or what I like to call "strengths waiting to happen").

*Being hard on yourself and being highly self-critical won't make you a better leader; it will only stress you out.*

Acknowledge your strengths, acknowledge your learning edges, and work from there. Showing up as a leader with self-compassion will soften the environment and help others to practice self-compassion too, and relax the "system." Self-compassion creates a space for growth. Being able to laugh at yourself in moments when you've made a mistake is a learning moment for everyone. One of the frightening things about change is that it is not known, so there has to be room for mistakes. Being gentle with yourself will show others how to be gentle too, it is also endearing. Charasmatic leaders are kind to themselves and others.

> *Mistakes point out what not to do next time, that's all.*

The more self-compassionate you are with yourself as a leader, the more self-compassionate your team will be, and the higher your level of psychological safety.[1] The famous scholar AmyEdmondson's research points to psychological safety at the heart of what makes a team most effective. Psychological safety is trust at the team level and the team's culture, allowing everyone to show up authentically and speak their minds without fear of being criticized. Psychological safety allows all voices to be heard, contributing critical data for finding the best way forward.

> *Be psychologically safe with yourself; drop the perfectionist hat, and adopt the learner hat.*

## Self-Care and Self-Compassion

Part of self-compassion is also self-care. I hear from leaders so often that they will rest or "do that fun thing" once this project is done. However, "this project" rolls into "that project," and before you know it, there is no time left for self-care. Self-care is not a form of pampering; it is a necessity. Self-care, like its counterpart burnout, doesn't happen overnight or with a day at the spa, nor is self-care about training hard for the next marathon (although it can be part of it). Self-care fills your bucket of reserves with things that increase your vitality and energy.

In general, leaders don't self-care enough (in my opinion!). Shift the conversation around self-care to understand that it is a proactive measure to fill your reserves. It is easier to keep your reserves than to lose or try to regain them; there is a momentum to self-care.

While there are some fundamental components to physical self-care, such as nutrition, exercise, and healthy sleep patterns, the nuances beyond this can be unique. This is true of psychological self-care as well. Having a sense of belonging, and meaning, are part of a healthy mind well-being, but it also could include psychological aspects such as following your curiosity, investigating new hobbies, expressing yourself creatively, engaging in a favourite sport, laughing with friends, often, etc. Developing a personalized self-care plan for your physical and psychological health is key.

> *Self-care is not a luxury. It's a proactive necessity.*

Use your equanimity to sit quietly and reflect on the following:

### **Reflection: Self-Care**

- What fills you up?

- What energizes you?
- What makes you laugh?
- Whose company do you enjoy?
- What sparks your curiosity?
- Are you doing any of the above now? If not, how can you incorporate them more?

# CHAPTER 9

# SPACE4EQ

- Self-Affirmation
- Inner Linguistics

> *"I saw the angel in the marble and carved until I set him free." –Michelangelo*

Words matter, and so too does how we talk to ourselves. Affirmations can help with acknowledging and shifting your inner voice to be more supportive and positive, which can profoundly impact your performance. In popular culture, the word affirmation has gotten a bad rap. I think of the funny character Stuart Smalley on Saturday Night Live! But in reality, affirmations play an important role in self-awareness and re-setting in a moment of equanimity.

- When was the last time that you acknowledged your inner voice?
- When you do notice your inner voice, are you using words that are positively or negatively charged?
- What do you affirm for yourself daily through the language or linguistics you choose?

- Are you careful in the way that you speak to yourself? And others?
- Is your inner voice kind to yourself?

Please pardon my multiple citations in this coming section, but I want to offer the science behind real affirmations! Too often, our inner voices are too critical, and we become our own worst enemy blocking our full potential. This is coupled with the fact that we sometimes like to be our worst critic. A tendency for hypervigilance and a binary thinking pattern of perfect or not good enough can be stifling. Affirmations help us to refocus our energies to be more helpful to ourselves. Our minds are so powerful, so it's important to be present with our thinking to eliminate the possibility of being a self-saboteur.

*Affirmations help to correct self-sabotaging efforts.*

Self-affirmation theory in social psychology has effectively acted as a buffer to stressful situations. Self-affirmations are simply about grounding yourself in all of your abilities and strengths instead of letting one stressful thing define your overall competence or define you. Self-affirmation is not about stating grandiose or ridiculous self-statements. It is instead about reminding yourself of all that you are and want to become in an authentic and realistic way.

*Words are powerful, and your body and mind listen to you!*

A self-affirmation intervention is a tool to anchor yourself in what is real and desired. It could be a simple sentence that grounds you, a mantra, or even a brief journal entry that affirms all you are instead of all you are not. By affirming the self in all you are, you decrease the strength of the stressful thing in front of you, whether that is an outraged client, an audience awaiting your speech, or a disgruntled employee.

Re-think how you talk to yourself and reset if necessary.

**A brief social psychological explanation.**

Self-affirmation theory in social psychology states that when an individual encounters a stressful event, there is an internal motivation to lessen the threat by maintaining one's integrity through other self-aspects.[1] Self-affirmation is a stress coping mechanism for reminding oneself of their *global adequacy* or all that they are.[2] It provides a buffering effect against stress and increases resilience. In addition, studies show that self-affirmation improves problem-solving under stress.[3] Self-affirmation interventions could offer a leader a useful self-reflective tool to increase their sense of personal competence and resourcefulness in adverse situations.

Using a self-affirmation intervention provides a leader with a way to increase their internal locus of control by focusing their appraisal of the stressful event inward toward their own level of capability. In essence, a self-affirmation intervention could help a leader untangle themselves or buffer against the event's stress by keeping their sense of personal adequacy intact for optimal coping.

When a threat is seen as less personally threatening, it will have less of an impact on one's stress level and psychological well-being.[4]

**Self-Affirmation in action.**

Let's look at fictious Rocky Robin and fictious Grounded Gray for a moment. Rocky Robin has always been self-critical. In fact, she believes, on some level, that being critical helps to keep her striving. Robin was taught how to be self-critical by her father, so she comes by it naturally. Robin expects the best of herself in any given situation but also never feels satisfied with her accomplishments. Compliments bother Robin and make her feel uncomfortable as though the person offering the compliment is trying to keep her at "that level." Failure is not an option for Rocky Robin, and her modus operandi involves a lot of pre-statements such as "I should…" Robin is constantly filling her resume with "shoulds." Before any sort of performance, Robin is very stressed because she feels that it has to be perfect. This strive for perfection is causing Robin to feel stressed a lot of the time. Robin has been so busy on the run, fulfilling the "shoulds" that she forgets what makes her curious and what she is interested in.

Now let's look at fctious Grounded Gray. Grounded Gray grew up with parents who suggested that he "follow his bliss."[5] Gray loves to try new things and feels comfortable in his own skin. Gray knows what his strengths are and wholeheartedly accepts what are not his strengths. In fact, Gray feels quite light-hearted about them. Gray seems to ease through life in a relaxed way, and there is an energy about him that is very welcoming and humble. Gray loves to pursue his interests and is clear on what he is truly curious about.

Again, we all likely have a bit of Robin and Gray in us, but wouldn't life be more enjoyable if we focused on our interests and authentic strengths and removed the treadmill of "shoulds"? This is not to dispel any obligations—it is important to discern an obligation or necessity (a "have-to" from a "should"). Being grounded within yourself is about being kind to yourself. Perhaps Rocky Robin could shift the dynamics of her stress and drive for perfectionism by taking time to reflect on what she loves to do, her authentic strengths, and then start each day with the reminder, "I am more than enough, just as I am," and "Life is about the journey."

Being kind to yourself as a leader allows you to reflect in the moment, accept your strengths, acknowledge (gently) when something isn't working and make the necessary course corrections.

**Self-Affirmation and Self-Care in Practice**

During my graduate research, my dissertation focused on developing a tool or intervention using a visual format. Traditional self-affirmations involve writing down and affirming what is true and valued for yourself, so I expanded on this by developing a visual format called a SPACE4EQ board. A SPACE4EQ board involves participants using Pinterest™ (www.pinterest.com) or any other online visual platform to select self-affirming images.

**Introducing the SPACE4EQ Board for Equanimity**

Stress and negative self-talk are the things that need to be shed, and affirmations help to reset and refocus.

The greatness of your mind can only emerge if you are free from its distractions and take care of it in a proactive way. Freeing your mind of your triggers, fears, hang-ups, negative defaults, stress, etc., while also giving it space to rest and renew, allows your ultimate cognitive performance to emerge.

> *If you are able to remove the distractions and intentionally chip away everything holding you back, your uniqueness is able to emerge.*

I am about to introduce you to a concise, simple, and creative practice to start a daily self-care practice that is mindful and aims to contribute to the development of equanimity. It may feel a bit trite at first, but I urge you to stay with me here; there is science behind it. It is similar to developing a virtual vision board, but with the focus of reflecting on aspects of self-affirmation, mindfulness, gratitude, positive emotions, optimism, etc., that are personal to you. Everyone has their own journey, beliefs, meaningful experiences, and sources of inspiration. The important element is to take ten minutes each morning to reconnect with everything that is YOU. The SPACE4EQ is a form of visual contemplation, and is a path to cultivating more equanimity.

I developed the SPACE4EQ board as part of my research. The constructs, which each are positive psychological interventions, include the following: self-affirming your stregnths, gaining perspective with positive emotions and gratitude, increasing optimism with a growth mindset, centering with mindfulness and nature, and untethering with equanimity.

## Psychological Self-Care for Leaders
# SPACE4EQ

**"S"**
Strengthening: Self Affirmations

**"P"**
Perspective: Positive Emotions & Gratitude

**"A"**
Attitude: Optimism & Growth Mindset

**"C"**
Centering: Mindfulness & Nature

**"E"**
Equanimity: Untethering & Composure

⬇

Increased Wellbeing, Decreased Stress,
Increased Ability to Keep Calm and Carry on

⬇

**Thriving Through Uncertainty**

## Developing your SPACE4EQ Board

You may already be familiar with Pinterest™, but in case you are not, I have laid out the simple steps in getting "onboard." Other online platforms could be used as well.

1. Log in and create an account, and I recommend setting your board creations to *private*, so be sure to click on the privacy setting.
2. Within Pinterest™, under "Boards," there is a plus symbol "+" or an "add" board. Here you can name your board—perhaps call it SPACE4EQ
3. Then, type into the search bar at the top of the page, any image you want to search for to select for your board. For example, if you want to reflect on a moment in your life when you were so grateful for a particular event, search the experience, "I was grateful for that morning when I woke up to see the mountains." You'll be surprised to see what comes up with "morning" and "mountains." You can even find a specific location, sometimes as focused as the coffee shop where you once had a beautiful morning. When you find an image that moves you or makes you feel and reflect, select the "save" button found in the top right corner of the image, and it should allow you to select which of your boards (you may create multiple ones) that you want to save it to.
4. At the beginning or the end of your day, sit in a quiet space, take a few deep breaths to begin your SPACE4EQ process, and be sure to turn off your smartphone and other distractions.

5. Just be with yourself in quiet for a moment.
6. In order to build your board, simply search for topics in the search engine, find the images that are powerful, relevant, and most meaningful for you, and click "save to your board."
7. Start with S: Strengthening and Self-Affirmation. Think about experiences, things, quotes, etc. that help you feel empowered, affirm who you are, or are part of your strengths. You will be amazed at the depth of images that are available, even back to something as remote as a camp you went to as a kid or your favorite coffee shop in a quiet corner of the world. Find meaningful images that are unique to your life experience that express this.

- What images depict your strengths?
- What images depict strengths you admire?
- What makes you self-affirmed?
- What helps you to feel determined?
- What fuels your spirit?
- What experiences made you feel brave?
- What experiences inspire you?
- What people, places, and things ground you and affirm all that you are?
- What's your Sisu?

8. Select as many images as you like. They don't have to be perfect, just ones that move you somehow or positively remind you. You can add more S images in the future. S also includes things that are part of your self-integrity, that help to affirm

all that you are and all that you want to be, in addition to your personal strengths or strengths that you admire in others.

9. The next day focuses on images that conjure P: Positive Emotions and Gratitude. For example, a favorite beach spot, song, or place to travel, or a sunset.

- What images depict what you are grateful for?
- What experiences are you grateful for?
- What will make you feel grateful in the future?
- What elevates your mood?
- What past experiences elevated your mood?
- What positive experiences do you want in the future?
- How does gratitude make you feel?

10. Then, the next day turn your attention to A: Attitude, Optimism, and Growth Mindset.

- What images help you to feel optimistic?
- What things help you to be open to learning?
- What experiences did you engage with a growth mindset?
- What will help you to be optimistic and open in the future?
- Who do you see as a good role model for optimism?

11. Then, the next day, focus on images that are C: Centering, Mindfulness, and Nature.

- Where do you go to get to nature?
- Where do you want to go to get to nature?
- How does nature make you feel?
- How do you practice mindfulness? Meditation? Art? Sports? Music?
- How might you practice more mindfulness?
- How might mindfulness make you feel?

12. Lastly, focus on searching images that represent E: Equanimity.

- What helps you to be equanimous?
- What might help you to become more equanimous?
- Who do you see as equanimous?
- What does equanimity represent to you?
- How can you increase your equanimity?

13. Now revisit your SPACE4EQ every day, even for five minutes, with the same routine of sitting quietly, taking a few deep breaths, being with yourself, connecting with yourself, and visually taking a tour of your SPACE4EQ. Some days you may want to just view your board. On other days, you may want to add to it. It's all about self-awareness and reflection and taking time for mind well-being!

### **Reflection: Your SPACE4EQ**

- How does developing your SPACE4EQ make you feel?
- Notice during the day if your SPACE4EQ has resonance?
- What stregnths have you remembered about yourself?
- How do you see and feel the SPACE4EQ helping you?

Personally, my SPACE4EQ is my reflective go-to. When I sit down at my computer in the morning with my cup of coffee, I visit my SPACE4EQ to set the tone of my day. Sometimes, I wake up feeling optimistic and ready, so I build on this by finding images to continue this mood, whereas some days, I might wake up feeling unsure or slightly overwhelmed, so I search for images to refocus my energy on positive things, places, and quotes. I consciously work to uplift my mood and then detach myself from the stressful state of feeling overwhelmed. I use my SPACE4EQ as a quiet, mindful, and reflective exercise in the morning to check in with myself to see where my mind is at and refocus my mind if I need to.

> *Ground yourself in YOU. Self-awareness, equanimity, and being able to center yourself within yourself—this is your superpower.*

## Next-Levelling Your SPACE4EQ: Best Possible Future Self

I would like to introduce you, also, to one more reflective exercise that is grounded in positive psychological research, with a SPACE4EQ twist! Dr. Laura King found that writing about your positive future goals is good for your well-being."[6] After you have built your SPACE4EQ board, then add an element of increased inspiration by selecting visual elements of what you feel your best possible future self would include:

- Where would you be?
- What would you be doing?
- What would you be feeling?
- What would your day look like?
- What would be on your reading list?
- Who would you be surrounded by?
- What will be your actionable items that day?

*Knowing **who you are** untethers you from all that you are not.*

The SPACE4EQ board can help collage what you want more of in your life or that which has inspired you; it is like a visual journal and vision board wrapped up in one. Use the SPACE4EQ as a way to reset, realign, and renew your mind and spirit each morning, in addition to the other aspects of your well-being routine. Use it as a launch pad for your day, for your intentions, and as part of your mind care.

*Reflection is a lost art, and yet it is a way in which you can center yourself.*

# CHAPTER 10

# Communication and Equanimity

- Navigating Conflict
- Listening

> *"What you do speaks so loudly that I cannot hear what you say." –Ralph Waldo Emerson*

Communication is more than words; it is a multi-sensory experience of one iceberg meeting another, two souls drifting through life, finding their way. At work, we all arrive at a meeting with our hidden hopes, fears, concerns, desires, etc. Still waters run deep in everyone. After all, we are all human. Words are powerful, but what is even more powerful in communication is the ability to listen and to seek to *really* understand the other with authentic curiosity. Real listening isn't just about *being quiet* while waiting your turn to speak. Instead, it's an intentional act to pause to be present with and understand the other; it takes the silence of equanimity.

> ***Silent and Listen have the same letters for a reason.***

Communication comes in different shapes and sizes; it can be anything on the scale of a simple message to something life-saving. Being able to effectively communicate as a leader in all contexts, especially while under pressure, is key. Equanimity is a friend to communication because it provides the think space, enabling you to collect yourself and be more present for the other when approaching any meaningful exchange. Equanimity is also aligned to being more empathetic, which is the ability to see and hear the other from the perspective of *their* story. If the other can feel truly heard, it will help provide a gateway for them to share more, increasing the quality of the dialogue.

### **Reflection: Dialogue**

- Take a moment to reflect on the last meaningful dialogue you had with someone. How did it make you feel?
- What were the important factors that needed to be in place to have that meaningful conversation?

When I asked myself this question, a long-time friend immediately came to mind. I can call her anytime with any issue, and she will be "in the moment" with me so that we can hash out the current seemingly wicked problem from all angles. I hope that I am that for her too. We might not talk for months, but one phone call or dialog, and we are fully reintegrated into each other's lives again. There is also a level of expected openness and authenticity, and we will tolerate nothing less.

Having a real conversation is about being in the flow with another person where the exchanges are both effortless and challenging simultaneously. Real conversations help everyone involved shed self-consciousness and permit all participants to think and speak *loosely* without the worry of judgement. Real communication is psychologically safe, meaningful, and intellectually stimulating, and usually, all parties walk away having learned something new about the other and themselves.

Easier said than done and contextually available, I know. However, keeping the ideal communication in mind when entering into a conversation is helpful. Equanimity can help you to contain the space by allowing you to use all of your senses and show up truly present.

> ***Real conversations involve next-levelling things instead of regurgitating the antiquated.***

**Communication and Uncertainty**

Communication during uncertainty helps team members to feel supported, improves collaboration, and it helps to increase trust. Thorough and honest communication also fills in any gaps that might lead to negative assumptions. Don't be afraid to overcommunicate in times of uncertainty, even if the only communication is simply "I don't know. Help me to figure this out."

There is a myth surrounding the need to be an expert if you are a leader. Some leaders feel that vulnerability and not knowing the answer is a sign of weakness and incompetence, but neither is true. In fact, it is quite the opposite. Vulnerability is brave; to show up in the face of adversity and outwardly acknowledge true emotions and a lack of expertise will open the door for the team to come together in a shared experience.

Something to remember, as a leader, if you don't have the answer, then, likely, neither does your team, so work together. Pretending like you know, even when you don't, will only make your team likely pretend that they have to know too, and bingo, lost psychological safety. Shed any useless notion that leadership equals expert-ship. Leadership is about learning and helping others to do the same.

Equanimity helps you to be okay with yourself and the situation, even when you are slightly afraid and unsure. Equanimity helps a moment be just that, a moment, and in turn, relaxes commmuniation.

## Conflict

Uncertain times breed stress, and stress can sometimes breed conflict. Coupled with the fact that conflict gets a *bad rap*, conflict tends to be something everyone wants to avoid, but it still seems to show up nonetheless. Quality conversations welcome respectful conflict because conflict is merely an expression of differing opinions. When faced with uncertainty, wouldn't it be best for the team if all of the divergent views could be openly brought to the table for consideration? Welcoming respectful and constructive conflict to the table takes a bit of navigating, but really all that it requires is deep listening and self-awareness from everyone.

If conflict arises within your team, the important starting point is for everyone to check in with their personal triggers and then find a shared common denominator as a starting place. For example, two team members may be miles apart on how they think the new product should be launched, but they can agree that they want it to be a success!

Commonly, both parties in conflict could *both* be right, so finding common ground for them to discover each other's perspectives with an open heart will help lead the way forward and even create synergy, where things are even more right. Setting the tone of the engagement with equanimity is critical. All parties need to identify what is irking them with calmness, open-mindedness, non-judgement, self-regulation, self-awareness, curiosity, empathy etc., then de-personalize the situation with the facts as much as possible.

The next time you feel or see conflict arising, slow the process down, formalize the conflict with a "perhaps we can take a pause here for a moment"…. and work to, gently, find out what is most triggering right to both parties. It is a great way to pause, reflect, breathe, and reenter a contentious engagement with a willingness to find a constructive and collaborative path forward. However, as a note, conflict needs to be handled with a gentle guidance, if one or both parties are in venting mode, perhaps guilding the pause to involve some space before re-entering into the conversation might be a more constructive start.

Here are a few fun facts about conflict to consider the next time you find yourself immersed in one:

- Conflict is normal, it happens in every group, and it doesn't have to be devastating.
- Conflict can lead to greater innovations by bringing forth many ideas.
- Conflict can help to identify something that needs attention, fixing, and healing—a pain point.
- Sometimes, conflict simply results from someone needing to be heard.

**Tolerance for Conflict**

Everyone has a different comfort level with conflict, and it can vary with situations. Contemplating your tolerances is a place to start. Ask yourself which situations are more triggering, what topics are more triggering, and alternatively, which environments are more calming. Some people almost seek conflict, and if there is conflict in the air, they dive in, whereas other people, on the other end of the spectrum, run for hills if things get heated. Most of us are somewhere in the middle, on a sliding scale. If you are a conflict ignitor, the next time you are in a conflict, try shifting gears by being the calm one. If you are a conflict-avoider, next time when faced with a conflict, try engaging in the heated discussion for a few more seconds, knowing that constructive conflict can result in something emergent and positive.

### Reflection: Conflict

- Think of the last conflict that you were able to resolve. What did it take?
- Think of a conflict that you haven't been able to resolve. What is missing?
- How do you feel about conflict? What is your tolerance for it? Are there situations that are more triggering?
- What can you do to expand your comfort level with conflict?

### Exercise: Conflict

The next time you feel a conflict arising, use your super skill of equanimity to pause, and ask yourself, what is our common ground, what do I need here, what do they need here? Then lead with that. For example, "I am hearing that we disagree on the strategy, but what we can agree on is the desired outcome."

> *"The difference between the right word and the almost right word is the difference between lightning and a lightning bug." –Mark Twain*

### The Power of Words

I've touched up the power of words in the self-affirmation section. Equanimity provides you the space to choose your words and how you *say* your words: wisely and with empathy for the receiving party. Understanding your communication style is important, as well as considering your audience. We all have blind spots surrounding how we communicate because we can't possibly understand how it is received by all.

Let's consider fictious Fast-talking Freda and fictious Shy Stella. Freda is always on the run and loves to get things checked off of her to-do list. Stella prefers to consider all information and processes things in a more methodical manner. Both are great at their jobs and are good-hearted people, but they work and communicate differently. Neither is better than the other. Freda will burst into Stella's office with excitement, wanting to get the ball rolling on things, and her speech is fast and loud. Stella finds this overwhelming and tends to shut down. Freda makes assumptions about Stella's quietness as though she is not going to move quickly enough. Stella assumes that Freda is too over-excited to see the details. This difference in working style causes tension in their relationship.

A coach is brought in to work with both Freda and Stella in helping them identify how their communication style might appear to the other, along with helping them to identify what is important for them to maintain. It is important for Freda to move quickly, and it is important for Stella to work on her own. Through coaching and using equanimity, Freda learns to put her thoughts into an email (because she needs to act now), but Stella can then read it when she is ready to (because she needs to act at her own pace). In addition, Stella has learned that simply responding to Freda's email with a commitment in response time, such as "Received with thanks. Will respond by the end of the day," is enough for Freda. Both Freda and Stella can now laugh about their different styles respectfully.

This is communication equanimity in action. Both have remained authentic to themselves while being cognisant of the other.

### **Exercise: Communication Style**

- What kind of communicator are you? Fast? Slow? Loud? Soft? Verbose? Direct?
- Start to take notice of your style and the style of others.
- How do your tone, pace, and style impact the quality of the exchange?
- Use your equanimity to play with your style in response to the environment for an optimal outcome.

# CHAPTER 11

# The Equanimous Leader

*Equanimity is like a bridge from yourself to the rest of the world, but you are the engineer of that bridge. You build that bridge with intention and only cross over that bridge when you want to, and in the way you want to.*

Equanimity is about grounding yourself from within so that you can become more authentically intentional with your thoughts, actions, and choices. Equanimity provides the space in between to catch your breath and collect yourself, especially in the face of adversity.

Stress can be a great resistor to the power of intentional creation because when we are tangled up in stress, we are fearful, exhausted, reactive, and distracted. Equanimity is about stepping the Self *up, or levelling up,* from a situation to get the full view. Make no mistake that equanimity is not about being detached; instead, it is about being at one with all of the Self in the moment and tapping into a deep inner calm.

Equanimity is the capacity for self-composure, self-awareness, and cognitive calmness, especially while under pressure. Equanimity stretches your reaction time by offering you a *stop-time* to check in with yourself, your reactions, your observations, and your decisions. In addition, equanimity allows you the *space* to be more intentional and less reactional in the face of uncertainty; a super skill needed by leaders today.

Throughout this book, I have identified ways in which to cultivate more equanimity as a leader:

- Self-Awareness
- Metacognition
- Stress Resiliency
- Gratitude
- Mindfulness and Meditation
- Nature
- Growth Mindset
- Sisu
- Optimism
- Internal versus External Locus of Control
- Positive Emotion
- Biases
- Thinking Errors
- Resilience
- Tolerance for Ambiguity
- Tension of Change
- Self-Affirmation
- SPACE4EQ

All of the above tactics can be incorporated into your day, week, and month to increase your capacity for equanimity as a leader, and they all involve self-kindness. It starts with giving yourself the permission, and time, to simply dial in, reflect in the moment, have a mind conversation with yourself, and breathe, deeply and slowly. Breathe slowly in, hold the breath in an effortless way for a moment, and slowly release it. Imagine yourself in the center of the vortex or the eye of the hurricane. Things will continue to "spin" around you, but stand still, collect your strength, separate yourself in a healthy way, and reengage in a purely intentional and not reactional manner.

Think of equanimity as a work in progress. It doesn't have to be a binary relationship of having or not having it. As you become cognizant of your ability to be equanimous, you might realize that you have this capacity in some contexts while less so in others. Contemplate what it is about certain environments that support you being able to keep your mind free and agile, and depersonalized unnecessary situations for a broader view. Equally notice the times when you are less able to be equanimous. What is it about that environment? What is the trigger that pulls you into the reaction of the moment?

> *"When force of circumstance upsets your equanimity, lose no time in recovering your self-control, and do not remain out of tune longer than you can help. Habitual recurrence to the harmony will increase your mastery of it."* –Marcus Aurelius

Part of the equanimous process is *also* about giving yourself permission to *not* be stressed. There is a weird myth "out there" about leaders needing to feel stress, as though it's a badge of honor, but let me dissolve this myth. This secret society or stress club of leaders is not one you want to join because they burn out. Have you ever heard of the expression "misery loves company"?

Instead, join the club of leaders who love to thrive, enjoy their life, be happy and energized, and want the same for their employees! An Equanimous Leader also has a fierce spirit, a calm mind, a clear heart, and an agile way. They are the captain of the sailboat who can right itself, and they are mindfully aware of themselves and others.

The inner illumination that can be sparked from a moment of pure equanimity as a leader will provide a space for thinking-freedom and wisdom. When our minds are tangled up in worry, tangled up in social comparison, thinking errors and false expectations, and needing to be a sudden expert all of the time, our minds can get stuck (less free). Equanimity helps to untether your mind from such weighty nonessentials.

Home is where your heart is. Your home is your center of gravity, within you, so don't give it over to the hungry vortex of uncertainty and stress. Hold it tight and steadfast. Anchor from within. Expect change. Be prepared, within, for uncertainty as a leader. Don't succumb to the stress epidemic. Instead, save your stress response for the moments when you really need it or can't help it.

Becoming an Equanimous Leader involves priming yourself with a practice of psychological self-care and cultivating a cognitive aptitude through mindful awareness. Lean into gratitude, meditation, art, music, exercise, sports, and nature in order to interrupt stress—this is your source of light. Ignite your bones by seeking positive emotional experiences, reacquaint yourself with your curiosities and strengths, and dig into your unbending courage to remember all that you are.

> ***Slow down, pause, catch your breath, and connect with yourself and your mind.***
>
> ***When you are good with yourself, you can be good with everything else.***
>
> ***Don't forget to enjoy the adventure!***

# ABOUT THE AUTHOR

Dr. Jennifer Signe Card is a leadership consultant, executive coach, and CEO of EQ @ HQ Consulting. Jennifer holds a doctorate in Organizational Leadership Psychology (Psy.D.), a Master of Science (M.Sc.) in Applied Positive Psychology and Coaching Psychology, and is accredited with a Professional Certified Coach (PCC) with the International Coaching Federation. Jennifer applies her passion for positive psychology and metacognition *(thinking about the way in which we think)* to leader, team, and enterprise consulting. She believes that a flourishing enterprise is built upon authentic collaboration in which people are empowered and have the *know-how* to show up as their Best Self. In addition, Jennifer believes that equanimity is a super skill of leadership.

# NOTES

Chapter One

1. Lama Dalai. (2001). *An Open Heart: Practicing Compassion in Everyday Life.* New York, NY: Little, Brown and Company. Page 162.
2. Edmondson, A. (1999). Psychological safety and learning behavior in work teams. *Administrative science quarterly, 44*(2), 350-383.

Chapter Three

1. Bono, J., Foldes, H, Vinson, G., & Muros, J. (2007). Workplace emotions: the role of supervision and leadership. *Journal of Applied Psychology, 92(5), 1357-1367.* doi:10.1037/0021-9010.92.5.1357
2. Dr. Aaron Beck (1963). www.beckinstitute.org.
3. Emmons, R., & McCullough, M. (2003). Blessings versus burdens: an experimental investigation of gratitude and subjective well-being in daily life. *Journal of Personality and Social Psychology. 84 (2), 377-389.*

Chapter Four

1. Kabat-Zinn, J. (1982). An outpatient program in behavioral medicine for chronic pain patients based on the practice of mindfulness meditation: Theoretical considerations and preliminary results. *General hospital psychiatry, 4*(1), 33-47.
2. Garland, E., Gaylord, S. & Fredrickson, B. (2011). Positive reappraisal mediates the stress-reductive effects of mindfulness: an upward spiral process. *Mindfulness. 2 (1):59-67.* doi:10.1007/s12671-011-0043.8.
3. Roche, M., Haar, M. & Luthans, F. (2014). The role of mindfulness and psychological capital on the well-being of leaders. *Journal of Occupational Health Psychology.19(4), 476-489.* doi:10.1037/a0037183
4. Capaldi, C. A., Passmore, H.-A., Nisbet, E. K., Zelenski, J. M., & Dopko, R. L. (2015). Flourishing in nature: A review of the benefits of connecting with nature and its application as a wellbeing intervention. *International Journal of Wellbeing, 5(4), 1-16.* doi:10.5502/ijw.v5i4.449
5. Kaplan, S. (1995). The restorative benefits of nature: Toward an integrative framework. *Journal of environmental psychology,15*(3), 169-182..

Chapter Five

1. Dweck, C. S. (2008). *Mindset: The new psychology of success*. Random House Digital, Inc..
2. Dweck, C. S. (2008). *Mindset: The new psychology of success*. Random House Digital, Inc..
3. Carver, C. S., Scheier, M. F., & Segerstrom, S. C. (2010). Optimism. *Clinical psychology review, 30*(7), 879-889.
4. Segerstrom, S. & Sephton, S. (2010). Optimistic expectancies and cell-mediated immunity: the role of positive affect. *Psychological Science, 21 (3), 448-455.* doi:10.1177/0956797610362061

Chapter Six

1. Rotter, J. B. (1966). Generalized expectancies for internal versus external control of reinforcement. *Psychological Monographs. 80 (609).*
2. Fredrickson, B. (2013). Updated thinking on positivity ratios. *American Psychological Association, 68(9), 814-822.*

Chapter Seven

1. Hefferon, K., & Boniwell, I. (2011). *Positive psychology: Theory, research and applications.* McGraw-Hill Education (UK).

Chapter Eight

1. Edmondson, A. (1999). Psychological safety and learning behavior in work teams. *Administrative science quarterly*, *44*(2), 350-383.
2. teams. *Administrative science quarterly*, *44*(2), 350-383.

Chapter Nine

1. Steele, C. (1988). The psychology of self-affirmation: sustaining the integrity of the self. *Advanced Experimental Social Psychology.* v. 21.
2. Cohen, G. L., & Sherman, D.K. (2014). The psychology of change: self-affirmation and social psychological intervention. *Annual Review of Psychology.* 65: 333-371. doi: 10.1146/annurev-psych-010213-115137.
3. Creswell, J.D., Dutcher, J., Klein, W., Harris, P., & Levine, J. (2013). Self-affirmation improves problem-solving under stress. *PLOSone.* doi:10.1371/journal.pone.0062593.
4. Cohen G.L., Garcia, J., Purdie-Vaughns, V., Apfel, N., Brzustoski, P. (2009). Recursive processes in self-affirmation: intervening to close the minority achievement gap. *Science, 324, 400–3.*
5. Campbell, J. (1987). Follow Your Bliss.*excerpts from The Power of Myth PBS interviews with Bill Moyers). Joseph Campbell Foundation.*
6. King, L. A. (2001). The health benefits of writing about life goals. *Personality and Social Psychology Bulletin, 27(7), 798-807.*

Made in the USA
Middletown, DE
06 April 2023